THE FUTURE OF WESTERN CIVILIZATION

PSYCHIATRIST DR NICHOLAS BEECROFT INTERVIEWS VISIONARY LEADERS

Series 1

Volumes 0, 1, 2, 5, 6, 7, 8, 9, 10, 11, 12, 13

BOOK ONE

The Future of Western Civilization:
Psychiatrist Dr Nicholas Beecroft Interviews Visionary Leaders
Series 1, Book 1. Volumes 0, 1, 2, 5, 6, 7, 8, 9, 10, 11, 12, 13

Western Civilization on the Psychiatrist's Couch
Oil Painting by Melanie Mortiboys Copyright © 2014

ISBN-13: 978-1494340070
ISBN-10: 1494340070

Book design by Maureen Cutajar
www.gopublished.com

Contents

Future of Western Civilization Series Mission

I'm Dr Nicholas Beecroft, a Consultant Psychiatrist in London. I'm exploring the Future of Western Civilization through a series of interviews. I want us to rejuvenate our energy, direction and self-confidence as a Civilization. My mission is to create a positive, appreciative space in which leaders at the evolutionary edge of our Civilization can share their experience and set out their vision for our future to inspire others. They are visionaries sowing the seeds of future transformation, all genuine, creative, courageous people who care about whom we are and where we're going.

By "Civilization," I mean Western Civilization-the one I've lived in; to one that is transformed the world over the last 500 years; the one that has gone global; the one that faces enormous threats, challenges and has the unprecedented opportunity to evolve to an amazing future. When there's so much changing all at once, old structures failing and a huge array of emerging threats, that all generates a lot of anxiety, pessimism and fear which distract us from putting energy into creating new solutions, generating new ideas and envisioning a better future.

Behind the News Headlines, usually quietly, under the radar, there's a lot of good stuff going on; the seeds of the future taking root in the present. There are lots of evolutionaries trying out new ideas, new technologies, new ways of organizing and more integrated, conscious and balanced ways of thinking and being.

Western Civilization has been supremely successful in all kinds of ways of which we should be enormously proud. Science, technology, industrialization, democracy, individual rights, personal freedom, property rights, the rule of law, Christianity, humanism, organization, capitalism, feminism, civil rights, philosophy, music, art, even Imperialism have all, on balance, transformed the world for the better and have created new life conditions with new challenges and problems. In some cases, these advances had nasty side effects and some have become imbalanced. In others, they have replaced older structures and beliefs, and many babies have been lost with the bathwater.

Human Civilization is made up of human beings who are conscious beings and physical animals, all interconnected like a shoal of fish or a flock of birds. I've interviewed a huge variety of people across a variety roles, professions, beliefs, politics, status, nationalities, religions, social classes and backgrounds. What is crystal clear to me is that whilst the world we live in is hyper-complex, we operate in it using a kind of mini-map of our Civilization in our minds which we use to navigate through the world, guided by our inner compass of intuition and rational thought. It is astonishing how similar these inner maps are, and the patterns are clear. This is how we self-organize in what is a complex living system-just like a beehive or wildebeest migration.

Now we are super-connected by the internet, media and travel. We carry in our pockets access to billions of people and to just about all the knowledge that ever existed. Turning inwards we have access to instinctive intuition, heart, wisdom, common sense and judgement. Put together, that represents vast human potential and the most amazing opportunity for personal and cultural evolution ever. Looked at like that, just about all of our shared challenges and threats are solvable and a much better world is highly realistic. We're engaged in conscious evolution of ourselves and our Civilization.

There is a huge range of threats and challenges to The West and to the whole World. People focus their attention on different ones depending on their situation, beliefs and emotional make-up. The list is pretty depressing and overwhelming-so I've turned it into a list of positive questions instead. Here's a start:

- Who are we?
- Where are we going?
- What kind of future do we envisage?
- How do we rise to the challenges we face?
- What do we believe; what is right, what is wrong, what is true, what is false? What do we value and desire?
- What do we love about our Civilization?

- What works well?
- What's worth preserving and defending?
- How can we be confidently patriotic, open, diverse and global at the same time?
- How do we restore a healthy authority in ourselves, our roles and institutions?
- How can we have authority which is fair, accountable, evidence-based and respectful of complexity?
- How can be apply science effectively to complex systems like the mind, consciousness, society without oversimplification?
- How do we get sustainable, secure, clean energy?
- How do we make the welfare state to be fair to taxpayers and empowering to recipients?
- How do we balance individual rights with group responsibilities?
- Shall we start having enough children to sustain our future without depending on immigration?
- How do we absorb huge flows of immigration into a confident, open, dynamic, cohesive and secure country?
- How can we be comfortable and secure with our complex, overlapping identities?
- How do we innovate, reorganize, get our way out of recession?
- How do we enjoy the growth of human potential in harmony with the planet upon which we depend ?
- How do we evolve capitalism to serve our culture and values more holistically and fairly?
- How do we rehumanize medicine to get the best of technology whilst having compassion and healing and open our minds to the huge non-linear, non-reductionist possibilities?
- How do we refresh our democracy to deepen it rather than have occasional elections manipulated by narrow interest groups, political cabals and the media?
- Who are successful examples of organic leadership-leadership in line with human nature including self-organizing living systems, trust, respect, judgement, intuition?
- What can we learn from pioneers in consciousness and cultural evolution?
- How can we most effectively support our cultural evolution, healthy attitude to risk, judgment and responsibility?

- How do we support the evolution for a more mature, more conscious post-partisan politics which integrates left and right, individual and group, power and love, freedom and security, justice and fairness?
- How can we integrate the dark, shadow side of our history so as to unlock our power and potential?
- How do we intelligently integrate what we have come to think of as science with intuition, wisdom and complexity?
- How do we preserve and improve our open, free, democratic, pluralistic society whilst living with other cultures which actively assert their righteousness, supremacy and desire for dominance over us?
- How do we rebalance our economies to live within our means, to support the development of the emerging economies whilst remaining competitive and vibrant?
- How do we live ecologically sustainably?
- How do we have a post-postmodern spirituality which honors life and spirit and which transcends and includes existing religions and secular views?
- How do we evolve from a culture of entitlement to a culture of empowerment, maximizing potential, freedom with fairness and responsibility?
- How do we emerge beyond patriarchy and feminism to a mature, conscious masculinity and femininity, embodied, equal but different, comfortable with our inter-penetrating Yin and Yang?
- How do we re-legitimize judgement; not prejudice but healthy judgement of right and wrong, good and bad as the foundation of autonomy, freedom and authority?
- How do we get healthy hierarchies which are empowering and adaptive?
- How do we create new fields of consciousness; our energetic potential into which the future will emerge-create the field of alignment and remove the obstacles and provide the support structures and allow the self-organization to occur?
- What's already here and happening...
- What new technologies are coming which will change our way of life and opportunities?
- What are the values and beliefs of emerging new generations around the world?

- How do we foresee or create the future?
- How can we boost our cultural direction and confidence?
- Where we are fighting, what are we fighting for?
- How can we make our Civilization so attractive that others choose to align with us, emulate us and synergize with us?
- What disruptive technologies are going to change our world?
- How can we live in harmony with the planet whilst continuing to evolve our way of life?
- How can we securely and confidently live with Islam at home and abroad while it goes through its turbulent period of evolution?
- How do we ensure that the basics of food, water, clean air, energy, health and education are available fairly to everyone?
- How do we evolve wrongs of racism, nationalism, imperialism without simply inverting them to become the future victims new racisms, nationalisms and fascisms from other cultures?
- How do we deal with growing geopolitical assertiveness and military build-up by China, India, Pakistan, Russia, Iran, Brazil, Turkey, South Africa?
- Can we make use of raw materials sustainably?
- How do we stay safe with continuing nuclear proliferation to Iran, North Korea and others?
- How do we clear our massive sovereign and personal debts and live within our means?
- How can we evolve the way we do welfare, health and social care to make them affordable and more supportive of a healthy society?
- How do we enjoy the benefits of capitalism without being debt-slaves and making sure we value family, community, health, environment, education, security, freedom and human potential?
- How can we rejuvenate the family as the cornerstone of our culture?
- How do great teachers inspire, empower and carry authority in classrooms?
- How can we compete with the very determined educational competition from the East?
- How do we bring in the alienated into the mainstream with dignity and compassion?
- How do we make taxation and welfare fair for hardworking tax-payers?

5

- How can we eat more healthy, natural food, connected to its production whilst making it fun and practical?
- How can we farm animals in a kind, healthy way?
- How can we make care homes wonderful, heavenly places full of life, stimulation and family?
- How can hospitals empower, support and care for their staff so that they, in turn, are fit to care for their patients?
- How can we value wellbeing over objects?
- Can we revalue fatherhood and motherhood?
- Can we value life and the human spirit in a way which is inclusive of all religions, spiritualities, humanism and atheism?
- How can our organizations maximize their human potential and help their team to live their purpose and values?
- Can we restore an innocent, playful, magical childhood?
- Can we reweave community by choice or is it something we only do when we have no choice?
- Who does empowering, inspiring, visionary, values-driven, spirit-kindling leadership?
- How do we balance our budgets and trade?
- ......And so on!

Acknowledgements

The Future of Western Civilization Series of interviews is the product of much work, many conversations and experiences over the preceding 30 years. Huge thanks to Melanie Mortiboys who has been fundamental to the project, it's conception, its incubation, birth and delivery. She has been there at every step of the way with encouragement, support, wisdom and good judgement.

The public face of the project, embodied in the series of interviews with visionary leaders got going in early 2011 with the first interview with William Nkata Masembe on the subject of patriotism from a newcomer's perspective. Many thanks to Nkata for being the first to boldly put himself on the line before the project was established.

Thank you to all those who took part in the subsequent Future of Western Civilization interviews: Melanie Mortiboys, Joseph McCormick, Martin Rutte, Dr Mary Gentile, Professor Jim Garrison, Dr Elisabet Sahtouris, Traci Fenton, Howard Bloom, Andrew Cohen, Dr Robin Wood, Chris Parish, Dr Don Beck, Herb Meyer, Neil Howe, Lynne McTaggart, Peggy Holman, Richard Barrett, Bishop Michael Nazir-Ali, Adrian Wagner, Joshua Gorman, Dr Robin Youngson, Jordan MacLeod, Mark Walsh, Soleira Green, Jim Rough, Joshua Gorman, Peter Merry, Helen Titchen Beeth, Barnaby Flynn, Danny Lambert, John Bunzl, Jon Freeman, Phil Neisser, Jacob Hess, Georgeanne Lamont, Peter Smith, Angeline Ruredzo, Steve Boley and Masana De Souza.

Behind the scenes, many people have been involved in the Future of Western Civilization project. Thanks to Linda Beecroft, Mike Beecroft, Cherie Beck, Dr Don Beck, Andrew Booth, Andrew Campbell, Chris Collins, Howard Donenfeld, Soleira Green, Samuel Humphreys, Jane MacAllister, Matthew McGuinness, Jan Mattsson, Hannah Mortiboys, Chris Parish, Martin Rutte, Lyndsey Wall, Matthew Wall, Dick Werling and Dr Robin Wood for their support and encouragement. Covers by Tatiana Villa. Formatting by Maureen Cutajar.

Dr Nicholas Beecroft

I'm a Consultant Psychiatrist. I trained as a doctor at Guy's and St Thomas's Medical School in London, doing a BSc. in psychology at University College as part of my medical degree. After a year as a House Physician and House Surgeon, I went straight into psychiatry at the Maudsley Hospital, the Institute of Psychiatry in London where I became a member of the Royal College of Psychiatrists.

I specialize in organizational and military psychiatry and have worked with the British Army, the Royal Navy and the National Health Service.

I spent 5 years developing an interest in what I came to call "Organic Leadership," aligning organizations with human nature to unleash maximum human potential. I developed this through a combination of consulting, coaching and teaching across a wide range of organizations including McKinsey & Co., BP, Cable & Wireless, the National Health Service, British Gas and Johannesburg City Council. I helped to establish the first Department of Organizational Psychiatry outside of the USA at King's College London where I taught executives and MSc. students Organizational Psychiatry and Psychology.

I have had a lifelong interest in Foreign Policy, national identity, security and geopolitics. Whilst I was at studying at the London Business School for an MBA, I watched the September 11, 2001 terrorist attacks live on television. This and the aftermath persuaded me that it was time to transform our Foreign Policy to include the human dimension-to perceive International relations as the interrelationships between individuals, groups and mass consciousness. I set about applying the knowledge and skills from clinical psychology, psychiatry and group dynamics to diplomacy and began to consult to diplomats, politicians and journalists. I called this "Psyplomacy."

I immersed myself in Track Two (off the record) diplomacy, helping to facilitate dialogue on immigration into Europe, the Weaponization of

Space, Western-Chinese relations, European Common Foreign and Security Policy, State-building, British-German relations, Public Diplomacy, peace building, Islamic radicalization and counter-terrorism.

I worked with the Foreign & Commonwealth Office in the British Embassy in Damascus where I put the British-Syrian relationship on the psychiatrist's couch, analyzing the relationship and recommending strategies to improve it.

I influenced the British Council in London to shift their model of public diplomacy from a marketing model to a relationships-based model grounded in a clear identity, values and authentic dialogue. They launched a new policy based upon the Psyplomacy model.

After the German Foreign Minister expressed his frustration at the treatment of Germany in the British media, he accepted my proposal to work with the German Embassy in London on a psychologically informed approach to public diplomacy to improve the British German relationship.

I helped to stimulate the debate within the British government and media about Britishness, patriotism and multiculturalism which is gradually been opening up over the last 10 years. I made a substantial commitment to work behind the scenes on our strategy for the "War on Terror" which I shared in a number of places including briefing two Foreign Secretaries, the Minister for International Development, the Conservative party, the BBC, Channel 4, the Ministry of Defense and the House of Commons Foreign Affairs Select Committee.

It became clear to me that, "We" the British and, more broadly, "We" Western Civilization had lost our direction and self-confidence. I began with a series of interviews with people which I called "Britain on the Couch." The key theme across the board was a perception of loss of confidence and authority. I interviewed teachers, doctors, nurses, military personnel and the general public to find out what is the foundation of their authority? What most fascinated me was that, in spite of coming from a very broad range of backgrounds, the people spoke as one as if singing from the same hymn sheet, I could almost sense and inner compass and map which everyone shared and-there was a big wobble in it! The traditional order and self-confidence arising from clear beliefs and shared identity had been breaking down but hadn't yet been replaced by a new set of beliefs and values. Culturally we have many old baggage and maladaptive beliefs which are limiting our full potential. If we going to succeed at a time of unprecedented global change then we can and need to step up to the next level of cultural and personal evolution.

I concluded that if we are to survive and thrive in the face of the many challenges which we face then we are going to have to sort ourselves out-to be clear about who we are, where we're going, what we believe, what is right, what is wrong, what is true, what is false; to restore our self-confidence, vision and values around which we can align.

I realized that to rejuvenate our society we would need a strong spiritual foundation. That was an uncomfortable conclusion for me because I considered myself to be undeveloped in that area. I was brought up to consider Christianity and spirituality to be a naive, unscientific, superstitious and rather embarrassing relic of the past which simply wasn't necessary in the modern world. However, through my explorations I realized that we need some core foundational truths about who we are as human beings, why we're here and how we should live. So, I set about a long journey of exploration through training in Energetics, Values analysis & facilitation, Transformative-Evolutionary Coaching, Vipassana meditation, Enlightenment Intensives, Tantra, Healing, Open Space Technology and Spiral Dynamics Integral. I participated in a Circle of Trust Courage to Lead retreat, the New Warrior Training Adventure, the Mankind Project, the Culture of Honoring Initiatory Journey and have attended many workshops on improvisation and comedy. The big questions are still largely a mystery to me but I'm a bit further forward in the enquiry.

There were three main conclusions that came out of all this. One was that for all the endless negativity in the media and public conversation about the huge range of problems and threats which exist, there are a huge number of people globally working on inspirational and initiatives, ideas and visions in what is a giant process of cultural evolution throughout emerging global consciousness. As Don Beck puts it, "No more prizes for predicting the rain. Its time to build the Ark."

The second main lesson was that it is a massive waste of time and energy when we resist that which we don't like. In a fierce battle with a Marxist professor which ended in stalemate, my opponent simply collapsed and dropped away when I asked him, "if everyone took up your ideas and if the world were the way you would like it to be, what would that be like?" He simply didn't know. He'd never considered it. He only knew what he was against, what he hated. He was like a windsock with no wind. I realized that to defeat all those cultural forces which I had so fiercely resisted, I simply needed to leapfrog to the other side with that incisive question. The only problem was that I couldn't answer the question myself!

The third main lesson was that we as individuals and a group have much of our power and potential locked away in our shadow, in our dark side, the wounds, the taboos, the dysfunctional beliefs, false dichotomies and the groupthink. To unlock our potential, we need to heal those wounds and shine a light on the dark side and integrate the healthy strands of all. The old false dichotomies such as left and right, male and female, love and power, freedom and control, security and openness, diversity and unity, cohesion and separation, judgement and non-judgement, truth and mystery, patriotism and globalism each have healthy and unhealthy strands which need sorting out and integrating into the whole.

In September 2011 I embarked on a project exploring the Future of Western Civilization to create a resource of interviews with visionary leaders at the evolutionary edge of our culture who can share their stories, experiences and inspirational vision is for the future. The aim is to play my part in rejuvenating the self-confidence and direction of our Civilization.

Introduction to the Series

Melanie Mortiboys interviews Dr Nicholas Beecroft

Melanie Mortiboys is a writer, artist, Pilates teacher, Bowen therapist, mother and Nicholas' girlfriend. She has been a key catalyst of the Future of Western Civilization behind the scenes, offering her wisdom, support, encouragement and judgement throughout. She studied Drama, Film and Television at Bristol University and has since explored the world of personal development, psychology and health. She is currently working on her first novel.

Melanie: You're launching a series of interviews with visionary leaders, tell me more about that.

Nicholas: We're at an exciting time in our cultural evolution. We can look at all kinds of negative things, all kinds of problems, but the point is that like never before as a species we are connected to others by the media, telecommunications and transport. We've got more knowledge, more information, more technology; more cultural openness than has ever before existed. That's a brilliant opportunity for cultural evolution. All of the problems that people can cite about where we are, and what's wrong, and so on are all incredibly soluble. Change happens in the first instance in our minds, by changing our consciousness with new ideas, new values and new attitudes.

The purpose of the interviews is several. One is to find those people who are at the evolutionary edge of our culture, who are already, quietly under the radar, doing things, creating the new seeds that will grow into great things in the future. Often they're not on the news, they're not known to the public but they're there beavering away and doing new things. We have many emergent leaders who are not yet in major positions of authority. There are some younger people, apparently on the edge, but through their creativity and through them stepping into their leadership, they are going to help us through difficult times.

Melanie: Nicholas, tell me more about what you're planning to explore?

Nicholas: I'd like us to, as a civilization, as a country, as a culture, have a real self confidence about who we are, where we're going, and what kind of future we're envisioning for ourselves. That starts on the inside. Who am I? Who are we? What do we believe? What's true and false? What's the foundation of our authority that runs through all of our relationships? I'd like us to feel patriotic, comfortably patriotic, at the same time as being global, open and multiracial.

Very clearly, we need to evolve towards a sustainable society; sustainable in terms of our energy, our food, and our raw materials. Medicine, I'd like to see rebalanced and become much more human, much more compassionate. Politics, in our country it's absolutely ripe to step up and get beyond the old battlegrounds of left and right, and the old ideologies to a much more integrated transformational place.

At the moment, globally, capitalism is in crisis. That presents a real opportunity, not to get rid of capitalism to go to some kind of utopia but to ask how do we evolve it to get the best possible value out of our investments and to value the full spectrum of human life and activity? Counterbalancing that, equally necessary, we must renew and refresh the welfare state. While it's essential that we look after the weak, and the poor, and the sick; we need to ask, how can we get the welfare state to have a culture of empowerment and not entitlement? How can it be fair for those who pay into it as well as those who receive from it?

I'd like to challenge some of the shadow parts of our history, some of dark bits from our past which are lingering in the background which, if we can healthily process, we can get beyond them for the benefit of our collective consciousness. Science is, again, an absolutely core and wonderful part of our civilization, but that too needs to grow beyond its very narrow foundation and actually begin to include intuition, consciousness, wisdom and collective intelligence into its broader form of knowing.

I'd like to explore how people are evolving and moving beyond the traditional forms of religion and spirituality, to try to distil a way of being which honors life, honors humanity, which transcends and includes the

13

previous and earlier forms of spirituality; because that is part of the foundation of goodness, and what helps keep us working together.

I'm looking for case examples of successful organic leadership in action. Examples of where leaders and organizations already work in line with human nature based on values, getting the best out of people, growing human potential and intelligently working with the grain of human nature.

Melanie: Why is this important to you?

Nicholas: I'd like to live in a culture, in a civilization that's self confident. Where we have a good idea of who we are, and where we're going; and people are engaging their full potential to take us to a better place. The purpose of the interviews is to have a space, a creative energetic, appreciative space in which the future and emergent leaders can put forward their vision, generate new ideas, inspire others, and also be challenged.

Melanie: Why is this necessary?

Nicholas: I think that the future isn't something which is predetermined. It's something which is emergent, it's happening all of the time; emerging through the complexity from where we are now. Although we can't meticulously construct the future, we can certainly influence it through new technologies, through new ideas. Fundamentally, everything comes from our consciousness, both individual but also collective, and in the space between us in our culture.

Why is it necessary? If we continue to focus as people do, naturally, on lots of problems all of the things that we don't like, all of the things that are not working, all of the problems that we have, all of the threats that we have; it's important to be mindful of those, to have the energy and desire to change. But if we are absorbed in those, that's a dead end. We need to put our energy into optimism, into new ideas, into new ways forward, and creativity, because that's where the future's coming.

Melanie: You used the terms, "Inner compass" and "big picture," what do you mean?

14

Nicholas: I mean that, human society, human groups, are groups of conscious animals. In the same way that a shoal of fish or a flock of birds all manage to move together in unison; people are very much the same. For example, a few years ago I was very interested in looking at authority, and how that was evolving in our society, observing that many of the traditional sources of authority and types of authority had come under attack in different ways, and a lot of people had lost confidence in the authority of themselves as a policeman, as a teacher, as a parent, or just in society in general. What surprised me was although I suppose it shouldn't have done, with hindsight, was that no matter who I talked to from those very different backgrounds they all seemed to carry a mini-map, and a mini-model of our society, of our culture in their minds. It was the same in everybody, and it struck me that actually that is brilliant because that means you can change it.

If we can change that mini-map in a positive way that takes off, that works, that's effective then, very rapidly, that will spread through each mind, like the shoal of fish or the flock of birds we will adapt to our life conditions.

Melanie: Do you think that there is a reason for hope amidst the pessimism of the present?

Nicholas: The future is not an extrapolation from the present; there are always unexpected things that happen. People adapt to their circumstances and change. People make different choices like, at the moment, suddenly people have stopped spending and are starting to save. That has not begun to feed through yet into a cultural change, but we're going to see that in the next 10 years. Until people change their behavior and their ideas you get new technologies that come through disruptive technologies which completely change the situation.

You get new players that come to the game. Most obvious at the moment; China, Brazil, these countries in the current circumstances are showing a lot more power and leverage than you could have imagined even 10 years ago. Events happen. 9/11 would be a classic example, but there are many things happening all of the time. Reasons for optimism would be that we can be creative, we can do things differently, we can

15

generate new ideas, we can invest in new technologies, and we can harness new technologies. Together we can use our collective intelligence to adapt, solve current problems and create a better world.

Melanie: Can we create the future by intention or just predict it and adapt accordingly?

Nicholas: My view is that the future isn't predetermined; it's not already mapped out. I think that the future is something that emerges from the present, and obviously the present is a very complex system with many variables. I don't think you can carefully manipulate things to get an exact outcome, but I do believe that we can influence the future by our present state, by our present mental state, our present culture, our intentions, our plans and our actions.

Melanie: You mentioned that you plan to offer appreciative interviews to the candidates in the upcoming elections. Surely they need tough cross examination by a Humphreys or a Paxman? (BBC political interviewers)

Nicholas: I think they definitely do need tough cross-examination by a Humphreys and a Paxman, yes, but I would say they need something else as well. For me, absolutely, politicians can be slippery, they want to move the subject onto things that suit them, they want to avoid those areas where they're weaker or not so sure about, of course. However, the thing that's missing in our media is an appreciative space, to give the person a little bit of time to spell out their vision of who they are, and where they're going, how they see the future, what the opportunities are, and how things would be if we followed their plans.

Of course, one needs to be disciplined and critical about that, but I think at the moment people are cut down so fast that they rarely get to say the positive stuff, and the visionary stuff. It's the visionary stuff which engages people's passion and energy, and that's what leads us forward. The lack of that is one of the reasons that our culture currently can be very cynical, very negative and switched off from politics.

Melanie: Will you always choose people with whom you agree on their opinions, or will that matter to you? Will you be able to interview people with whom you don't necessarily agree?

Nicholas: Definitely. In fact, all of the interviews I've done so far are with people I don't agree with! The world's got seven billion people, as of last week, so if we only stuck to people that we already know, that's a definite route to failure.

British Patriotism

A Newcomer's Perspective

William Nkata Masembe

Dr Nicholas Beecroft interviews William Nkata Masembe on his perspective on British Patriotism as a Ugandan who has come to live in London. He describes those things that he loves about Britain and the British and gives his observations on how multiculturalism is working. He loves the tolerance and diversity which Britain offers, particularly in London, but he feels that political correctness has suppressed what ought to be a healthy patriotism and celebration of Britishness whilst being fully global, multiracial and inclusive. Nkata is a Psychiatric Nurse working in London. He maintains close contact with Uganda including an active engagement in politics. Within Uganda, he identifies as a Bugandan.

Nicholas: Nkata looking from your experience in Uganda, you have lived over here in Britain for quite a while now....

Nkata: Yes.

Nicholas: How can we healthily and safely, positively and optimistically manage immigration, nationality and identity?

Nkata: My view is two pronged. One, it could be managed or, two, we can let loose and fail to manage it until we get chaos. Chaos where the immigrants are coming from and chaos where the immigrants are going. For example, you find yourself these days that Africans, the educated ones, are rushing over to Europe and now some Asian countries. The gap they create back home is amazing.

Nicholas: You can't make them stay at home, can you? You didn't. You didn't stay at home.

Nkata: No, but I am sure there are a few things which policy makers can do together with international ones, especially at points of destination to ensure that gaps are not created, but also where these people come so they don't overwhelm people.

Nicholas: You said something about there being a link; you feel an empathy with white working class British people or some similarity with them.

Nkata: Yes.

Nicholas: You were talking about some similarity with them. Could you say a bit about that?

Nkata: I felt empathetic because of the sense of being overwhelmed by new experiences of which they were never part of in the making, but which were imposed upon them. There are similarities I see with, for example, from where I come from in Uganda. The host is being antagonized; the host is being disrespected, the host is being demonized.

Nicholas: The host being Bugandans?

Nkata: No, the host could be Bugandan, the host could be M'choli, the host could be Nkole, Kalamojongs, Basoga, etc. I am talking about those nationalities within Uganda.

Nicholas: How do you see that playing out in Britain?

Nkata: In my observation we have situations where people have been labelled as being extreme right just because they have expressed a view of how things should be and shouldn't be. Just because they have expressed a view about the trauma and of their scary experience of immigration.

Nicholas: If a white person expresses anxiety about the nature, degree, speed, etc. of immigration does that make them a racist?

Nkata: I always say that is bollocks that that shouldn't be the case, it shouldn't be. People have got the right to express, to say, what they have to say because there is a reason why they need to say it.

Nicholas: What is the difference between being a racist and being someone who is a healthy patriot?

Nkata: I think a racist is someone whom you would say is less informed of the experience of the other and the views of the other, who takes one line and follows that through without cross checking and without having a dialogue, without having an understanding what the other's view is. We also need to be very mindful of not suppressing and not stopping those people from expressing aloud why they behave as they do, why they think as they do and why they behave so towards others. I think the word "racist" is loosely used. It is very emotional and people jump on that bandwagon of emotional weakness to grab political points to justify their existence.

Nicholas: Who is doing that?

Nkata: I could say that because I'm an immigrant from Uganda that anybody who is indigenous white, whatever they are going to say at work I can attribute that to being racist. That is common in workplaces.

Nicholas: You mean you can use it as a weapon?

Nkata: As a weapon. It's a weapon. It's a weapon.

Nicholas: On the positive side though, you said that you are kind of British in a transactional way, having a passport, but it's not in your heart as such in a way that being Bugandan is. As someone who has lived here a long time, what is a healthy British patriotism? What is there to be proud about in being British?

Nkata: The inclusiveness. I have been around Europe and the inclusiveness around Britain is unprecedented in other countries. That makes you feel that people can hold on what they are and they believe in, but continue to live together and do business together. The fact that people can come here and explore opportunities. Unfortunately, sometimes, we look on the simple, minute human problems and we capitalize on that and come up with conclusions that we are not being accommodated fully, we are discriminated against. I think there is a lot to celebrate.

When you look at the way systems operate, there's been many improvement in human relationships and opportunities to immigrants. That is something to celebrate. If you ask me, as someone in transition, is that something you wish Uganda should be? Very much so, but what I would hate to see is that there is a systematic way of trying to tell me that I shouldn't be proud of being of a Bugandan, I shouldn't be proud of being a Nkole, Kiga or Mugisu.

Nicholas: There are people in this country who have suppressed the British identity, saying it's all racist or its imperialist and we need to be global and open and to suppress our own identity, but to celebrate others' identities. You're saying that we can have it both ways. You're saying that it is wrong to crush and denigrate the indigenous identity, but you're saying also it's really great as a newcomer to be really welcomed. Is there a way, in the British context, for us to be healthily patriotic and open to newcomers and allow newcomers to remain in their hearts whom they are without having to fake a British patriotism if they don't yet feel it?

Nkata: That is a hard one, but I think we should encourage the newcomers to appreciate the host and ways of life of the host and celebrate with the host.

Nicholas: (laughing) I am laughing because that is difficult to do in an era when we have unravelled all of our own identity and structures and thrown them all up in the air. Finally, what's your vision for a future Britain in terms of identity, tribe, belonging, being open to newcomers and being global?

Nkata: Celebrate our differences together. We can. Global is not a new thing. It has always been global. I will give an example the King (Kabaka), King Mutesa the First of Buganda in the late 1880's wrote to Queen Victoria requesting Her Highness to send him teachers of alien and new knowledge he thought would do good to his subjects, and that was global business, to send him teachers. After so many years now most of the education we have is grounded in that strategic and foresighted thinking by Kabaka Mutesa the First. Business can be done, we can help our people think of and identify areas of life we can celebrate our differences, we can celebrate our identities and people should be left to live and learn to learn new ways of living with others naturally without being coerced by ideological thinking and social constructs of the state or some form of dictatorship.

Nicholas: Great! Thank you very much for that.

Nkata: Thank you.

The Next Big Shift

From Machine to Living System

Dr Nicholas Beecroft

Dr Nicholas Beecroft describes the evolution of our culture from a materialistic machine into being a fully conscious living system. This is the transcript of a speech given at the at the 21 Century Network in 2011. The question posed to the speakers was "What's the Next Big Shift?" in our culture and society.

My answer to the question, "What is the big shift?" is to say that it's already here, and it always has been here. We are living beings interconnected in a web of relationships which is part of a living system. The big shift that we're just beginning to go into is to consciously acknowledge that, to believe it, and to act as if it was true. I'm going to say a bit about cultural evolution and then I'm going to give some examples of the living system in finance, in medicine, leadership, and technology. Then I'll say a little bit about a cultural strategy to speed up the transition.

The future is already here; it's here in many little seeds in lots of different places, many different people. They're little bits of the future, and we can choose what future we look at depending on the lens through which we want to look. If we look through a fearful lens, anxious about the breaking down of old structures, worried about our security then we're going to see a different future than if we choose to look through the evolutionary lens.

We're now at an amazing moment where we've had hundreds of years of Western Civilization which has provided us with the most amazing successes. Of course, it also created new problems as all advances do. The great advantage we have now in moving forward is that, for the first time because of the internet, because of media, because of travel we actually have a global consciousness emerging, and like never before we've got the ability to learn at incredibly high-speed from each other across time and across space.

If we're going to adapt to this new environment, one of the first shifts is going to be within. I think we've been very good at using our left cerebral hemisphere; linear, logical, reductionist, objectifying thinking, which has been brilliant in providing science and technology, etcetera. If we are to go forward into a living-system way of being then we're going to have to use a bit more of the right brain; a bit more interconnection, a bit more vision. We're going to need to be more conscious in using our instincts, our hearts, our gut, and our subtle interconnections with others.

There's also a rebalancing going on a global scale. Since Imperial times, people have been going out all over the world, but now we're really learning from the East things like equilibrium, mindfulness and consciousness. From India, we can learn the ability to live in diversity which we're going to need to do more so. From Africa, we're just beginning to learn how to tap into our wisdom and self-organizing governance. The remaining few hunter-gatherer societies have got so much to teach us about knowing ourselves, knowing our instinct and knowing how we live in nature.

In medicine, we've been stuck in the technical and bureaucratized way of operating, and that has had many negative impacts. We are just beginning to turn the corner. For example, recently, I was talking to a surgeon who is working on the surgical guidelines from the National Institute of Clinical Excellence, which produces clinical guidelines for the British National Health Service based upon evidence based medicine. They're just beginning to add into the surgical guidelines an awareness that surgeons through their training actually carry, embodied knowledge, both conscious and unconscious in their bodies, which they're using moment to moment during their operations to make judgements, take decisions, assess complex situations, weigh risks and so on.

In my own field, in psychiatry, obviously we have to assess suicide risk. The bureaucratized technical approach that has taught clinicians that we can't trust judgement and intuition. Increasingly, we are expected to tick lots of boxes and fill out audit-able checklists. When you speak to people privately they tell you that they go through the motions of the protocols and box-ticking, but in parallel, they also very much read their gut instinct. We use our senses and our multilevel awareness in judging someone's suicide risk. We use the rational, logical reasoning and combine it with our animal instincts, though that is not officially valued.

Look at the way we do leadership, for another example. It's crazy that we seem to run our National Health Service (NHS) as though its Stalinist, centralized bureaucracy, or like a Ford machine. Of course, we know that's not true. You've all seen the shoal of fish or a flock of birds, seeing how huge numbers of individuals manage to align themselves, and that's what the NHS is. It's an amazing system of individuals; each one a cell containing a map of the whole, guided by their inner compass.

Clinical governance, shouldn't just be a pack of files that you stick in a cupboard, a pile of policies that no one ever reads, except the auditor when they come around. It's something which is embedded in every individual consciousness, and every interaction between every doctor, every patient, every nurse, everything constantly, mostly unconsciously or semiconsciously.

It's not long ago in our own culture that this was taken for granted. I was really heartened when I went on holiday to Istanbul, and visited the Selimiye Barracks where Florence Nightingale ran her wards during the Crimean War. On the wall, there's an inspiring letter. There were a group of nursing students who were arriving at a time when she was away somewhere else, and so they had to arrive, read the letter and then get on without her for two weeks. Now you have to cut her a bit of slack because it was written in pre-political correctness times, and times have moved on, but the underlying principle remains the same. The first page says, "A good nurse is a good woman. A good woman has the following characteristics: kindness, compassion, self-discipline, fortitude, care," et cetera, In other words, a long list of values and virtues.

Then the second page said, "A nurse's job is to care for the sick and to carry out doctor's orders." An absolutely clear statement of task. A clear statement of values, statement of task then enacted by a group of people who are working well together, communicating effectively with a clear vision, with appropriate training, support and resources. That's the basis of organic leadership.

Technology is perhaps the area we most associate with materialistic, reductionist science. I'm sure many of you know that it's opening up to what's called biomimicry. We're not just taking medicines from nature, we're finally really learning from nature, asking nature, "How do you make an adhesive?" or "How do you make an incredibly resilient material which is very strong and flexible?" We're just at the beginning of that and it's yielding amazing results.

The final example is finance. How is finance a living system? We're all familiar with the caricature of the greedy banker driving around in his Porsche, cruelly riding roughshod over the poor people and of the very soulless calculations of return on investment and analyses of risk. That's true, but anti-capitalism is a dead-end. It's not going anywhere. I think that the way forward is for us to create a new field, a new vision, into which capitalism can grow.

So if you imagine, sometimes you see a picture of the globe upon which an airline will draw the lines around it where their flights go or Cable & Wireless show will show where their telecommunications go. If you imagine in your mind's eye what it would look like if you could see the flow of capital from people to banks, to investments going around like an interconnected system. Then if you rethink what is money, capital. Capital is a store of human energy. That's all it is.

An investment-what is that? That's a group of people. That's human potential. You can begin to imagine how seeing capitalism as a living system might work, capital as human energy flowing seamlessly from place to place into human potential, serving the whole of life. That might sound wishy-washy and idealistic, but it's already beginning to happen. People are already experimenting with ways of measuring value more broadly including different types of values. How does investment have an impact on upon family, on security, upon the community, the environment, the culture and so on? People are beginning to experiment with the structure and ownership of companies, so they don't only consider the shareholders and the government, but they look at other types of stakeholders.

What cultural strategy should we have to catalyze this evolution from the materialist machine model to a conscious living system? Ultimately, we don't really need one because it's happening anyway and it's going to happen anyway. That's the nature of a living system, but we can speed it up. I think we can do that with all of us being leaders in our own way. It doesn't have to be politicians alone. For ourselves, we have to calibrate our inner compass, practice mindfulness, being aware of ourselves, our values, our truth, our power, what we believe in, and crucially bringing that to the web of relationships in which we interact.

We can bring our awareness to those people with whom we intercon-nect and ramp up the energy, and you do that by tapping into what you care about, and creating beautiful new fields, visions of what we want to create. Ask incisive questions. If you have the kind of world you would like it be what would that be like?

Finally, in summary, I think the next big shift is very simply that we're going to acknowledge that we are living beings, interconnected with other living beings in a living system, and act as if we believed it, reaping the benefits of being closely aligned with nature.

Global Simultaneous Policy Making

Bottom-Up Global Policy

John Bunzl interviewed by Dr Nicholas Beecroft

John is a businessman with a simple and powerful new vision for global governance. In 2000, John Bunzl founded the International Simultaneous Policy Organization (ISPO) and launched the Simultaneous Policy (SIMPOL) campaign; a campaign that allows citizens to use their votes in an entirely new way to drive their governments to act together to solve global problems.

Ever since the campaign started John Bunzl has worked tirelessly to reach out to citizens, activists, non-governmental organizations, politicians and business people to raise both their awareness and understanding of what global simultaneous policies could mean for humanity, prosperity and peace.

John Bunzl is a passionate speaker on global consciousness and on simultaneous international action, and their relevance to a wide range of topics: from tax justice, the regulation of the financial markets, sustainability standards, fair trade, military spending, to global warming and more.

John is a regular contributor for the Huffington Post, and has spoken at TEDxBerlin, TEDxGoodEnoughCollege and at events facilitated by organizations such as the World Social Forum, The Schumacher Society, the World Trade Organization, and at various universities including the London School of Economics.

You can contact John via Twitter, LinkedIn or www.simpol.org

Nicholas: Welcome, John.

John: Thank you. Very nice to see you.

Nicholas: And you. The reason I've invited you today is that I'm really fascinated with the work you've been doing over the past few years and would really like to hear what your vision of the future for our civilization is.

John: That's a big question. I think my vision is really a continuation of the evolutionary idea that we've moved from tribes to Middle Age small states to nation states, and now we're fiddling around with things like the European Union, the United Nations and the World Trade Organization and the various quasi-global bodies, but what we're actually struggling towards is a cooperative global society, or I would say, global governance, but stressing governance rather than the government, because they're two quite different things. We're working our way towards some sort of global governance, which is cooperative, which would be an international coordinated action rather than a global government per se.

Nicholas: If the ideas of SIMPOL that you put forward were working really well, could you describe what it would be like?

John: Yes, I think what it would be like would be a nation's implementing policies simultaneously, such as the Tobin tax (a proposed tax on financial transactions), such as corporate taxation and regulation, but it would be rather like income taxes at the national level where the rich pay more and the poor pay less, or even the very poor would pay nothing at all, there would be compensations between different nations.

I think this is one of the real barriers to cooperation we're seeing at the moment, if you look at things like climate change or what happened at Copenhagen, the world is trying to solve its problems one issue at a time, but of course on a particular issue, each individual country wins or loses. The big losers on the climate agreement would be China and America because they've got the most to cut so it's not surprising, that there is no cooperation. If you mixed two issues together, for example, a climate agreement and have the Tobin tax, the funds that you raised from the tax you could use to pay off the big losers on the climate part of the agreement. That's a very crude example, but until they start putting two or three issues together so that what nations may lose on the swings they can gain on the roundabouts, you'll never, ever, ever begin to get cooperation and that's the bunfight we see in Copenhagen. It's not rocket science, really.

Nicholas: What does SIMPOL stand for?

John: SIMPOL stands for simultaneous policy. That means, effectively, it could be any desirable policy that nations can't implement alone because they fear jobs or investment moving elsewhere, so they need to implement simultaneously with other nations. In principle, if everybody implements them simultaneously, all nations win. If you include corporations, there will be a level playing field, if you'd like, with appropriate compensations and swings and roundabouts as I've just described.

Nicholas: Is your idea that this runs in parallel to the current organization of nation states and United Nations and so on, or this an alternative structure?

John: It's essentially an alternative structure, but works through national electoral processes. It works through the system, but it's not of the system. That's very important, because there's no point creating any kind of alternative structure, which is to alienate it from the existing system, because then you're just creating something in competition with what's already there. The whole point about SIMPOL, simultaneous policy, is that it's evolutionary, it's transformative, it actually works through the system and I can explain, if you'd like, how that works.

Nicholas: Yes.

John: Basically, let me just back up a little bit and just explain that if you look at very many of the things today that people are concerned about, democracy, climate change, and banker's bonuses, financial system, all of these problems are problems which nations cannot tackle on their own. For example, if any nation tried, as many monetary reformers say we should, to take the issuing of new money back into the hands of the state and out of the hands commercial banks, any nation that tried to do that on its own would just see the banks going elsewhere and jobs going elsewhere. If any nation tried to implement higher emissions cuts, it would make business less competitive, jobs would be lost, simply because nobody wants to move. It's a vicious circle, and all nations are playing the same game.

Simultaneous policies sounds incredibly utopian in a sense, until you really understand this competitive road block, this vicious circle that all nations are caught in, which actually means that it's not simultaneous policy that's utopian, it's the system that has so dreadfully out of kilter that we need something like simultaneous policies to bring proper democratic accountability to the financial system and to the banks and to our environments and all the rest of it.

I didn't really explain to you how it works, did I? When you realize that, as a citizen, your vote isn't terribly meaningful anymore, and I think this is what the protesters, Occupy Wall Street, and all the way back to the protests against the World Trade Organization back in the nineties, are concerned about, that the political process doesn't permit them to change things anymore. The reason for that is because all nations are competing with each other. They have to keep their economies internationally competitive, which mean they have to all implement the free-market, centre-right agenda. That's why Old Labour becomes New Labour. Politicians are now bunched up in a generally centre-right position from which they can't escape, and that means that policies which fall outside of those narrow parameters are impractical because they are the policies which if a nation implemented them alone, it would become uncompetitive. Well that's impractical, so it just falls off the agenda. Democracy is what I now call pseudo-democracy. It doesn't matter who's in power, even if we voted a Green party into power, the Green party will still find that it will have to keep the UK's economy internationally competitive. That would mean jettisoning essentially the core of its agenda.

That's the first point; we realize how our votes have become meaningless and that's terribly depressing. "Oh my God, what do I do?" is actually the first liberating step, I would say, because when we realize our vote's meaningless, we can actually say, "OK, we can turn the tables now." We realized that all these policies that we need on climate change, on financial markets, all these things are absolutely necessary, we now know governments can't implement them alone, so we'll make our own policy and we'll call it the Simultaneous Policy to be implemented by all nations simultaneously so nobody loses out. People can support it before it gets implemented, because it obviously can't be implemented until everybody's on board. What we will do, is we will turn around to our politicians and we'll say, "You know, Mr. Politician, I will be voting for any politician or party, within reason, that signs up to implement the Simultaneous Policy alongside the other governments." If I have a preferred party, I want my party to sign up to it. The whole point of saying "any," is of course very powerful because when the politician comes knocking on your door and says, "Dr. Beecroft, would you be voting conservative?" or "Mr. Bunzl, would you be voting Labour," I turn around and say, "actually, I'll be voting for any party within reason that signs up to the Simultaneous Policy." The immediate question a politician says, "What's the Simultaneous Policy?" The energy is turned immediately around, 180 degrees. Instead of us lamely choosing these manifestos from these political parties, which we all know but cannot solve anything, we are now making our own agenda where we can force them to compete with each other to adopt the Simultaneous Policy.

Nicholas: I suppose for that to happen it's got to be something that's exciting and accessible for ordinary voters who generally are not particularly into politics. What's going to light the fuse to generate excitement?

John: I think it will take time. For people to get interested in something like SIMPOL, they have to develop a more world-centric awareness. Even a lot of people who are protesting, are still more in a nation-centric level of awareness because the whole idea of protest, for example, assumes that there's someone there who can deliver what it is you're protesting about. Governments can't deliver it; this is the point. There's no one in the cockpit. This is what we've got to realize. When we open the door, there's no one in there. That's why we have to get in there ourselves with our own policy, our own agenda because destructive international competition determines that no government can deliver what the protesters would have them deliver.

Let me just come back to the way that our supporters are voting and talking to politicians because that process of the last general election actually resulted in 200 candidates from all parties, mostly Liberal Democrats, and even a few Conservatives signing on and of those, 23 are sitting in Parliament. The number of us it took to achieve that, I don't dare tell you because it was so few. That demonstrates the incredible leverage we have.

Nicholas: That sounds very undemocratic.

John: In some ways, it is, but in a sense, Simultaneous Policy can't get implemented until all nations are on board and therefore, in a sense, in the beginning it's like a tin opener on the political system. Yes, it could be described as a bit undemocratic but ultimately, nothing can get implemented until sufficient people and nations are on board. There's no real undemocratic danger to it.

Nicholas: Other than the examples you just gave about the last election are there any examples of where SIMPOL has taken off in maybe small seeds or little examples?

John: Not really, because in a sense, this is a global unit. It's unprecedented because we're talking about people-centered global governance effectively, and of course that's never happened before. If you think about it carefully, Simultaneous Policies happen all the time. If a law is past at Westminster to do anything to change the tax system or to make any kind of reform at all, it's implemented globally in the sense of being implemented across the entire nation and it's implemented simultaneously in the sense that it happens across the entire nation on a certain date. If we have an election, it's on a certain date, the polls close at a certain time. It's global and simultaneous because otherwise, you get free riders or you get problems. The principal that we're talking about is as old as the hills; it's not actually anything new. That's quite encouraging, rather than it being something untried and untested on the global level but actually if you want to go into the biomimicry and ...

Nicholas: I'd love to.

John: You do? You could go back to prokaryotes and eukaryotes.

Nicholas: Go on and describe that.

John: If you read, for example, evolutionary biologists such as Elisabet Sahtouris or John Stewart, we're made of nucleated cells. Cells with a nucleus. Prokaryotes were full of organelles inside the cell which were also competing with one another and eating each other up until the cells died. At some point, so the story goes, one organelle within the protocell, what became the nucleus, started to somehow orchestrate a process by which it said to all the organelles, which over a millennium had competed themselves to death repeatedly, started to invite them to contribute some of their DNA to what became eventually the nucleus. If you wanted to link it to Simultaneous Policy, you can almost imagine that this is the nucleus saying to the organelles and the corporations and the governments, "What would be your policy, your DNA, for the new world, the new cell we all want to have to survive?" They all contributed their ideas and at a certain point, so the story goes, suddenly, the competition flipped from competition to cooperation. At that point, the nucleus became the key governing organ of the nucleated cell, which is the cell that then went on to being able to produce multicellular organisms by themselves.

You can call this fractal biology and it's repeating patterns in biology like a fern in which each little bit on the leaf is similar to the inner branch of the leaf, which is similar to the whole leaf. It's a repeating pattern, and I think in a way, simultaneity, it's going to be the only way on this planet that we can actually align each nation's or corporations into certain individual interests with the global interest.

Nicholas: Going from the cellular level to the global government, there's a massive step! Are there any other stages on the way where something like SIMPOL is already working, like in a family or in a school?

John: Yes, for example, it's in the family. I don't know if you've got kids or if any of them smoke, but if you want to implement a no smoking rule, there would be no point whatever to say that they can't smoke in this room, but they can smoke in that room. You'd still get the smell. There'd be no point in saying that the family can't smoke, but visitors perhaps can smoke. You have to have a global and simultaneous governance, because otherwise, the whole purpose of the rule is undermined.

Nicholas: That sounds the opposite of evolution, because evolution is based on many organisms all doing their own thing and competing and adapting, there's new mutation, new ideas, and the successful ones take off and the unsuccessful ones fall away.

John: That's true, and natural selection is very important. You tend to only see the cooperative side in human societies and also things like bees, beehives, ant nests, in non human life. It's less obvious. Governance in nature is more because of the competition. In other words, the lion will eat the weakest of the gazelles. That governs how many gazelles there are and it also subtly governs how many lions there can be. In human societies, you can say that all animals will exploit their environment and expand to the extent of their capabilities or the extent that they're not hemmed in by the governance provided by competing species.

With humans, of course, we're so much more powerful, so we end up having to govern ourselves. Of course, if we fail to govern ourselves now at the global level, we're finished. We're absolutely finished. There's no doubt about it. In a sense, you can say that governance has evolved up to the nation state level, but of course the economy and the environment and global warming already gone world-centric; they're already up at the world level. There's a tension, there's a governance gap between the nation-centric governance and global governance. The question is how do we do that?

Nicholas: The current attempts at global governance would be the United Nations, the World Health Organization, European Union, NATO, and so on. How does what you're putting forward with SIMPOL differ from or add to those current models?

John: I would suggest it probably because it's the only one that will work. Let me explain. The UN, for example, is effectively a club of nation states; it's created by nation states and the only organ within the UN that has any real authority or power is not really the UN itself, it's the Security Council, which is the world's most powerful nation states. That's an inherited contradiction in the UN. For the UN to evolve into a form of binding global governance, the most powerful nations would

35

have to cede power and authority to the UN. That is the last thing they're going to do, obviously. The UN is not going to bring global democracy to the world, the world will have to use something like SIMPOL to bring global governance and global democracy to the UN. That would be my guess, because the way SIMPOL works through national electoral processes in the quite powerful way I have explained, gives citizens in democratic countries a chance to take the initiative to get that process rolling and to drive politicians and governments towards a position where they have agreed in principal to cooperate and to implement policies simultaneously, if, and only if sufficient others do likewise.

Nicholas: John, what was it that got you into this? What made you personally passionate and put all of your energy into this?

John: (laughing) A complete mistake! Honestly, I was having Sunday lunch with my family and we were just, as you do, talking about this and that, global warming, and the world's falling apart and what are we going to do, and da da da ..... I was doing the washing up afterwards and we were carrying on the discussion. My mother turned around and said, "What would you do about it?" I had this flash of insight, "It would have to happen simultaneously, because unless it did, you'll always have a free rider come through or you'll always have the cooperative aspect that's required but always be undermined by somebody else." If you talked about simultaneous implementation, nobody need to lose out. I think the point is that although when we talk about that today, it sounds quite utopian. That's because the water, the level of need, the level of calamity is still fairly low at the moment; I wouldn't agree, but in the general public's mind, there's the sovereign debt crisis and there's global warming, but it's still living comfortably. We're still functioning reasonably. So the water level is still at our ankles, but when the water level gets up to here, (up to the neck) then the need for cooperation becomes obvious. Of course we'll do it, because if we don't, the water will go a little further. What we perceive as being in our best interest today, will be quite different I think when the water gets a little higher.

Nicholas: We can perceive this process bottom-up or top-down. We can look at it as an emergent living system process, which grows from the bottom up and just happens though all the different fractals, all the different cells, and it's just a naturally emergent process. One legitimate criticism I've heard is to say that to get that kind of coordination, you either require everyone to agree, which is rather unlikely, other than on a tiny number of things, or you have to have top-down control. There's a real risk of authoritarian government.

John: I think that actually, if you look at the probabilities, the 90% probability is that we'll go down the tubes; there will be total breakdown and chaos. Let's leave that aside, and look at just the 10% chance. If we assume that we're going to survive, there's got to be some kind of global governance and I think unless people get with a democratic people-centered, bottom-up movement like SIMPOL, what we will end up with is what we're talking about, which is authoritarian governance that is brought in terms of state of emergency, the corporations and the governments put together their version of global governance and we won't like it; it'll be pathological, it'll be authoritarian. That's exactly where we're headed, barring a collapse. If we don't get behind something SIMPOL or something very similar.

Nicholas: The outcome hangs on and where power lies.

John: Yes, that's right. Let me give you another example. During the financial crisis in 2008, when the whole sub-prime mortgage thing started in America, interestingly, at a certain point there, all the world's Central Banks, Western Central Banks, cut interest rates by half a percent simultaneously, because they realized that unless they did it simultaneously, it wasn't going to work; it wasn't going to have any effect. At the same time, China wasn't in on the plan, but the People's Republic of China Bank came in and did it as well because they thought, "Good idea, we'll all do it together." Then it'll have an effect. That's an example of simultaneity in action. That's my argument that as pressure rises, the pressure for cooperation rises, is it democratically informed? That wasn't. That's an example of governments getting, or central banks getting together to impose something together, which may or may not have been beneficial. Who knows, I'm not an economist. That's the danger that that can happen. That's why we need a citizens movement for global governance, which is practically what simultaneous policy is.

Nicholas: In the last year, there've been a couple of really big grass roots movements-the so called Arab Spring and the more recent Occupy Wall Street protests that have gone global. What's the relation to SIMPOL, or what does SIMPOL learn from that?

John: I think the Arab Spring is really more the level of consciousness of rationality breaking out finally in the Middle East, where people are no longer prepared to accept mythic or authoritarian mythic governance from an Ayatollah or a Gaddafi, or from whoever it may be. "Come on, we can run the place ourselves; we don't need some Ayatollah to tell us how to do it." That's rationality breaking through. That's hopefully democracy breaking through. It'll only be pseudo-democracy, they don't know that yet, but it'll only be pseudo-democracy because they'll find that this great democracy that they fought for, to the extent that they're part of the global market, as they will be, they'll find that it's just as empty as our kind of democracy. It's actually pseudo-democracy because their government, too, will have to keep its economy internationally competitive, depending on whether they've got oil wealth or not and all the rest of it.

Nicholas: It sounds like what you're saying can only come about if the life conditions are so extreme and so desperate that people are willing to go for it.

John: Hopefully, they won't get so desperate that we're going to collapse, but things will have to get a whole lot worse before people realize, before people's consciousness moves from nation-centric to world-centric and realizing that we'll actually have to have some form of global governance and that if the citizens don't jump up from the back seats of the plane to get into the cockpit, the politicians and the banks and the corporations will jump in there first. I think that's the danger. It'll be simultaneous, it's just a question of who gets there first. I would rather that we the people got there first and not our corporate friends.

Nicholas: John, you've been leading this for a long time now, and no doubt you're very used to questions, criticisms and challenges. What do you think the most challenging challenges are to SIMPOL?

John: By far, I would say, it's the evolution of consciousness. It's the evolution of people's cognitive and spiritual development from a nation-centric to world-centric. For example, you'll see a lot of people calling for a new paradigm, and then the next thing they say is we need to actually change the existing system through a nations; that we've got to get our government in this, and they completely miss the point. The whole point of a new paradigm is that the existing paradigm doesn't work anymore. I think it was actually David Cameron who said recently that the biggest surprise to him when he became the Prime Minister was that he pulled the lever and nothing happened. That's because the national levers don't work anymore. Hello? All the power is up in the global space now, and the biggest barrier to something like SIMPOL is people not yet really understanding that we have to have some global system and understanding that the problems are now global. It is no longer within the power of the nation states to influence to any certain significant degree. That's a big leap for people to take; when people take that leap, SIMPOL is second nature to them.

Nicholas: What other legitimate criticisms or challenges to SIMPOL are there?

John: The most obvious question people say is you can get politicians to sign up for SIMPOL, but then they won't implement it. The answer to that, of course, is that because SIMPOL only gets implemented when sufficient nations are on board, there's actually nothing politicians to renege on up until the time of implementation. At any point up until implementation, if a politician signed up, why would he have signed up? He would have only have signed up to win the SIMPOL vote, which could make the difference between him winning or losing his seat. If he reneged on SIMPOL, obviously, he's in danger, he's inviting the support he garnered to desert him. So, "Do I want to cut my own throat?...No." There's no point in anybody reneging. The only question is, would politicians renege once you've got all governments on board once you got all the people behind it, once you got the problems lined up. I don't think anyone is going to think about reneging because it won't be in anybody's interest to renege because the advantages of cooperation will have become, by then, very obvious, and it's not obvious today.

Nicholas: Why should existing centers of power, like companies, centers of capital, military powers, various cultural power groups, why should they be interested in giving up their existing structure and power and going over to what you're talking about?

John: I think, Nick, because it'll increasingly be in their interest. Even today when you look at the Occupy protest, for example, here and there, you see quite a number of bankers coming along. "Actually, I kind of agree with these guys, but I'm caught in this system; I'm a banker, I didn't chose to be a banker, but I am a banker, so I do what I do, but I understand what they're talking about." I'm a businessman too; a small businessman. I don't run a big corporation. Businessmen are not stupid, and actually, businessmen, they know. I think this is, in a way, why I came up with the Simultaneous Policy, because I'm a businessman. I know about competition, I live and breathe competition every day of my life. I know how destructive it can be, as we often say, if we don't do it, our competitors will. If Shell doesn't ruin the Niger Delta, it knows that Texaco will only be too happy to take its place. Corporations are stuck in a bind as well, and I think ultimately there will come a point where they too will realize that this is not in anybody's interest. They want to be in business for the next fifty years, not just for the next three. I think there will come a time where the existing centers of power will realize that it's in their interests to have some kind of global regulation than none at all, because having none at all is just going to throw us all over the edge.

Nicholas: How do you know that what you're saying about SIMPOL, the way it works, the vision, the need for it, how do you know that it's true? You said it's the only way that it would work, how do you deeply, honestly know this?

John: I said that slightly tongue in cheek. There may be other ways that things can work. I don't know, of course I don't know, but what I do know, Nick, is that we've tried it out in the UK context for the last five or ten years, over the course of two or three general elections. We know it works. We've got supporters in about seventy different countries. We're most advanced in the UK, but since party political competition, whether it's proportional representation or whether it's First-Past-the-Post, the principle is competition between political parties. That's the only condition we need for SIMPOL to work. It can work more powerfully probably in a First-Past-the-Post system than it would in a proportional system, but nevertheless, it can work in both. I don't know if what I'm saying is true, but it works, there's some evidence that it works.

Nicholas: Would you mind giving a few examples? You said we know it works in the UK, can you give a few brief examples of those?

John: Yes, the example that I like the best, actually, which did my heart good and is really what I would like to convey to the Occupy people, for example, was what happened in the last election. I think it was in Weston-super-Mare, the constituents in Weston-super-Mare, where at the previous election, I think the Conservative sitting MP had won by only about 150 votes, so it was a very marginal seat. It took just one of our people in that constituency ... I try not to say this, but I'm saying it on camera ... it took just one of us to write to all the candidates. Even the Conservative signed up, because he knew that, "If I don't sign up, but my Labour competitor or Liberal Democrat competitor does, and if there's a few more of these SIMPOL people in my constituency than I realize, I could lose my seat."

Nicholas: Have they kept their word after the election?

John: When they sign up, it's in writing. We have the signed pledge in my file. What was really nice about it was our supporter chap down there who had written the letter, he emailed me and when I told him the news that he had signed up and the pledge had come in, he said, "Oh that's great, now we can get all of these buggers," it was that feeling of empowerment. "Now at last, we can take back control." That's what I'd like to convey to the Occupy people is that actually, you don't need to freeze your arse off in a tent outside St Paul's Cathedral, you can do it in a much more subtle way through the vote, but that's a hard sell at the moment, because people are running away from politics, and what I'm trying to say is, "Wait a minute! Number one, we won't do this without politics. Number two, with SIMPOL, we've got a way we can do this, which is actually incredibly powerful." It's a hard ask to call them back because we all know everybody's running away from politics.

Nicholas: Some people might listen to what you just said and say, "Oh my God, who is 'we?' Who is this secret organization, these dark sinister forces, (both laughing) who are manipulating the system?" What types of balances are there to make sure that if SIMPOL really took off, that it wouldn't be dominated by small interest groups or powerful individuals, and would generally be fair and democratic?

John: Yes, first of all, what I've been talking about with the voting process is just the political process part of SIMPOL. The other part of SIMPOL is the policy development part of SIMPOL. What is the Simultaneous Policy going to consist of, what policies is that going to consist of? On that, there is no policy at the moment. The policy is being developed by anybody who signs off to the campaign, so everybody, if they sign off on the campaign, has an opportunity to get involved in proposing and refining and developing and voting upon the policies that they feel are important but the policy development process is strictly democratic, number one.

Number two, nothing can get implemented, as I said, until all sufficient nations are on board. Number three, SIMPOL only exists through citizen support, so if something were to happen, if I were to, or if some officer of SIMPOL were to be caught with his trousers down or something disastrous or have his hands in the till, or was doing something underhand, people would cancel their support and SIMPOL just goes "Poof!" It just ceases to exist.

Nicholas: How can you have global governance run from the grass roots when the world is so diverse, there's so many different types of people in different countries with different life conditions, different priorities, how can that be realistic?

John: Good question. Let me explain that we have a two-stage process to policy development. The first stage is that supporters in each country have their own independent national policy development process. People in the UK, for example, in our own process here, which we've already started in the UK, we voted climate change as the top issue, financial market regulation was number two, I think. We've got a process in each nation where from each country's or each national citizenries, national perspective, what are the global policies we feel to be most appropriate. SIMPOL supporters in every other country will be doing the same thing.

The second stage, and the second stage would only commence once there's a lot of political support and there wasn't so much question of if but when we would start implementing something, then the second stage would be a global negotiation where all the SIMPOL groups and even governments from non democratic countries would come together to thrash out the final set; that would be where all the tradeoffs and where all the haggling would go on between nations about who gets what proceeds from the Tobin tax and who has to cut their emissions.

That's the second stage, so that's how you would marry the diversity, which is very important that that comes into the process, and then end up with the unity in the second stage. It's easily said, of course, but I don't know exactly how it would unfold, but it seems to be something along those lines would be what might be workable. I think the other point is that not every policy qualifies for Simultaneous Policy because it can only include policies which nations can't implement alone. For example, if someone said, "We'll have Simultaneous Policy on capital punishment," if an individual nation implemented capital punishment on it's own, would it cause itself a significant competitor disadvantage? No. The whole raft of cultural or ethnocentric level policies, if you like, that just don't even qualify, so I think that also helps to leave the field clear for those policies that we really do need, like financial markets, corporate tax, global warming and so on.

Nicholas: The last niggling doubts are around the basics of human nature and in the balance between competition and cooperation. If we think of a queue of people there'll always be a balance between the desire to queue for fairness and the desire to push to the front of the queue. In any system there'll always be freeloaders, there'll always be selfish people, there'll always be cheats, and there'll always be people, say, "I can't bear the slow process that all these people are involved in, I'm just going to go and do my own thing." How does your vision for SIMPOL accommodate those factors of human nature?

John: I think there will always be those people, and on one hand, if that natural instinct or that propensity was that powerful, then we wouldn't have nation states; we wouldn't have had Middle Age small states, we wouldn't have had any form of governance at all, but we have, which indicates to me that although those propensities and tendencies are there, they're not so all-pervading that they completely destroy cooperation. The other point that I tried to get across earlier, is that you're asking me that question from a position of today where the pressure for cooperation is actually fairly low. When the pressure for cooperation becomes very high when the crisis gets very apparent, people's view of what's in their interests changes. A lot of people think cooperation is about self sacrifice. No, it's about self interest but you need the conditions to be right. It just depends how the life circumstances tilt things over from competition being in our self interest to cooperation being in our self interest.

Nicholas: If anyone reading would like to get involved in SIMPOL, how can they do that?

John: They can just sign on as a supporter or an adopter as we sometimes call it, which they can do at www.SIMPOL.org. It's free, because it's a democratic process, a democratic right, and your democratic responsibility. That's all you need to do, the minimum what we ask people to do is at election time to write to their politicians accordingly and we can help you with that. If you want to get more involved in campaigning or starting local groups, we've got local groups starting in different constituencies, that is there to be done too, so there's everything to play for.

Nicholas: Thank you very much, John.

John: Thank you.

The Future of Capitalism

Getting What We Really Want

Jon Freeman interviewed by Dr Nicholas Beecroft and Melanie Mortiboys

Jon is a Director of the Centre for Human Emergence in the UK. In the interview, Jon lays out his vision for the future of capitalism. He describes the shift in values we need to make to relate differently to money to put it back in its place as our servant, not the other way round. He is informed by his deep knowledge of Spiral Dynamics which he describes as an upgrade to the human "operating system." His manifesto succinctly sets out the challenges and limitations of capitalism. It doesn't prescribe particular strategies but rather posits some basic principles and values which might guide us in our debates about how to evolve it for the better.

After being European IT Director for a market-leading multinational, he has spent almost three decades in change and program management as a consultant to some of the UK's largest businesses. He has deep understanding of the systemic aspects of personal and organizational change. He works with organizational transformation, and as a leadership and relationships coach.

His book "Future Money: Evolving our relationship with finance" articulates the personal and systemic shifts that will be required for a healthy and sustainable monetary and economic future. His most recent book "The Science of Possibility: Patterns of Connected Consciousness" completes a 25-year quest to present a comprehensive narrative that marries science and spirituality. It is unique in its breadth of coverage, embracing biology, evolution, physics and cosmology, providing an evidence base for alternative and non-ordinary reality. It offers a powerful and exciting vision of the potential for human existence rooted in both evidence and personal experience.

Jon's SDi introduction can be accessed through www.che-hub.com and his books are on www.spiralworld.net and also available through www.lulu.com/spotlight/jonfreeman

Nicholas: Jon, this month you've launched a Manifesto about the Future of Money, the Future of Capitalism. It's a vast subject, covering an enormous range of things, but, could I challenge you to summarize, what's the core essence of it?

Jon: The core essence of the Manifesto is that we have a financial system which clearly is not working any more. Capitalism has been alright with some weaknesses up until now, but it's showing signs of having reached its use-by date, and we need Capitalism Mark II. So, what the Manifesto is about is an upgrade to the human operating system, and specifically in the financial arena.

Nicholas: What would be the best way to make decisions regarding finance, for us all?

Jon: There's a few different answers to that. The first is to shift the balance between central decision-making and local decision-making, so that there is much more accountability to local communities, and much more representation of the needs of local communities, or regions, in decision-making.

The second is the shift away from the high level of influence that corporations and financial institutions have on the way that governments think. Now, that's happening partly because of who has the ear of government and who has the clout to buy lobbyists, and it's partly a mindset which buys into this, "Oh, it's the money that's important, not life that's important", so that the various voices which would represent other aspects of life are seen as secondary, a sort of, "Oh, yes, we might need to think about the environment a bit, but it's not the important thing."

Actually, all those various stakeholders in our lives need to have an equal voice.

Nicholas: What would make decision makers make that reorientation towards life over money?

Jon: There's a few different answers to that too. One is a shift in us, and the way we vote, because at the moment we vote according to what we think will benefit us financially, and so there's a huge amount of manipulation of taxation, and so on, which is kind of about governments giving us what they think we want, and what we currently think we want, whereas actually what we want is to be happy, and that isn't necessarily about money, but we don't know how to express that yet, fully.

So, some of it comes from us, and changes in how we think. Some of it will come from increased education of our politicians, so they actually understand how the money system works, which currently very few of them do, such that all the things that I've said in the manifesto about debt money, that would be completely incomprehensible to all bar about five or six of our current Members of Parliament (MPs).

And then, we should create more of an open space to where there are other conversations going on, which our politicians can hear, and which educate them in the stuff that they're not yet seeing.

Nicholas: Jon, part two of your Manifesto challenges us to learn to live within our means, and to democratize money. Can you say a bit more what you mean about that?

Jon: Well, the two things go together, because when you look back at the story about debt money, and the way banks are injecting all the money into the economy, that's partly driven by our own individual decisions, not to live within our means but to borrow from the future, and it's also driven by governments' decisions to do likewise, so there is a shift from that point of view. We also have to stop the banks creating that money. They should never have been allowed to do it in the first place, because money supply is a fundamental of our national economic life. The principle is that the government should actually be controlling the money supply, and for as long as the banks are not regulated within a framework that controls that, then there's no accountability back to what's for the benefit of the country and its people, like you and me and everyone else.

So, we need a mechanism which sets up an independent monitoring of what's needed in the money supply, which is managed independent of the government, so they can't go out and buy elections as they might otherwise be tempted to, but which is managed on behalf of the people, accountable through Parliament ultimately, and filled with people who don't have vested interests.

Nicholas: Something that's become really obvious is that the system has become so complex, that even very senior people like the Governor of the Bank of England are struggling to understand the system, and what's going on. What can you do in the decision-making body that you're talking about, to make sure that they can deal with that level of complexity?

Jon: I think that the advantage of the scenario I'm describing is that the bit that they're required to manage is moderately self-contained. They are only required to manage the money supply; they're not required to manage everything that then happens with the money in the consuming economy.

Nicholas: When you said about money being created by banks, you were talking about the 3% that comes from the government, and the rest is expanded by the banks effectively creating money electronically. Although there are current problems, there's no question that the whole world is radically more wealthy than ever before, and although we've got this current blip, what makes you so sure that we need to get rid of that system, rather than just creatively find a way out of the recession, and get on with business as usual?

Jon: Well, we're wealthy in a certain sense, and there are a lot of real goods being produced, which we are all benefiting from in our lifestyles. But from an economic point of view, there's all sorts of things which aren't working. One is that we massively owe money in various places for that. Another is that we aren't able to manage our planetary resources, and we know that that's got some payback time, and some things that we've got to deal with, like peak oil and all of that.

So, yes it is working, and I'm not suggesting that we should destroy it. It's about modifying it so that we are able to manage its many challenges; to create the balances that it needs.

Nicholas: Point three of your Manifesto is that we need to replace speculation with real economic growth. Could you outline what you mean by that, and why it's necessary?

Jon: Yes. When 97% of the money that's being pumped into the economy is unreal money, it's just figures in computers which don't represent something real and tangible on the planet, then it's very easy to get into a mindset where you think that as long as you're growing those figures in computers, you've created something, so people get the idea that you make money out of money. That wasn't the way that money was originally used. The way that money was originally used was that you put it into some productive activity, and out of that productive activity, you created a service, or you created some goods that enhanced human life. Just growing money doesn't actually do anything to life itself.

So, we've gone into a free lunch mentality, collectively, where we think we've made a gain when we do speculation, and we grow money on pieces of paper, and we've invented some very complex instruments by which to do that which nobody understands, and which everybody knows are part of what got us into trouble. So we need to stop doing that. We need to have constraints on speculation, and there's some good solutions already out there like the Tobin tax which we could certainly use to put a brake on it. We need to have separation of banks that hold and manage your and my money from financial speculative investment vehicles which should be allowed to fail. It should never happen again that these are seen as too big to fail, and are bailed out with your and my money. That's a proposal that's out there but it's not being implemented, because the banks have persuaded the government to hold it back.

We need a fundamental shift of mindset which takes us back to the place where the purpose of investment is to put money into the productive economy, so we that we can do things better and create more ourselves. The 8%, which is all that currently goes from the banks into the productive economy, simply isn't enough, and the 92%, which is going into fueling property bubbles and speculative ventures is far too much. It's unbalanced, and it's unhealthy.

Nicholas: What is that 8%? You mean industry?

Jon: Out of the money that banks create and lend, only 8% goes into what you could define directly as the productive economy. It's much cheaper and easier for them to lend to you and me, regardless of whether we can truly afford to pay it back.

Nicholas: The thing that you referred to, the Tobin tax, that's the proposed European Union tax on financial transactions, is it?

Jon: Yes.

Nicholas: It sounds to me that there's a couple of problems with that. One is that it's actually a brake on the economy, because that isn't necessary a brake on speculation alone; that would be a dampener on all financial activity.

Secondly, the issue that that would disproportionately affect Britain, because Britain's economy is very biased towards the financial services industries, and it would put us at a disadvantage to competing economies.

Jon: Well, there's a couple of things in there. The first is to say that the government is very protective of the financial services industry, because, supposedly, it generates 15% of our economy. The trouble is if you look at the fact that that 15% consists largely of money that the banks themselves have created, that is not entirely real and not entirely beneficial, so then it may not be so good to maintain that way of working, it may actually not be in our interests.

It's also about the nature of the transactions themselves. A lot of the transactions that make the economy unhealthy are generated by computers in milliseconds, and so there's huge volumes of that which are going through the system as part of the speculative economy, which really dwarf the day to day real transactions which might be involved in lending to a business, which wouldn't be significantly impacted.

Nicholas: Jon, part four of your Manifesto says that we need to deal with the high level of inequality, and move towards a system that has much more fairness built into it. Could you describe why you feel that's important, and maybe outline your proposals to improve it?

Jon: It's a question of balance, this one; it's not because I have any kind of belief that inequality either could or should be eradicated. It's actually quite right that people are rewarded for their entrepreneurial flair, their hard work, their inventiveness or whatever. People should be able to have an incentive for making that choice of lifestyle, but what's been happening in the last couple of decades has actually gone way beyond that. There's been an increasing shift of the nation's wealth into the pockets of a very small minority-into the 1%.

The result of that for everybody else is to create a great deal more struggle, and that has repercussions in the quality of our social lives. It has repercussions in the way that our ability to fund all the social services and our needs for social services occur. It doesn't work as a social whole.

Nicholas: What's your vision of how things could be much better?

Jon: How things could be much better is, firstly, that corporations are expected to pay taxes in the countries where they operate. They are actually expected to participate. Then there's the lower level of all of that, which is, again, the operation with multiple stakeholders, that the planet is a stakeholder, the environment is a stakeholder, customers, suppliers, employees, the wellbeing of the surrounding society, all of those are stakeholders in the business which a corporation is required to manage. It doesn't all come down to something which is narrowly measured as profit. That doesn't mean that profit isn't also a stakeholder. Yes, you have to be able to return money to your shareholders if you've got investors, of that kind. They're stakeholders too, but they are among many.

Nicholas: So, if companies are expected to measure their benefits, value, activity, etc., according to a much broader range of values beyond the financial, who's going to be the person or system that arbitrates between competing values?

Jon: My view of that is that it needs to be done internally. I don't think you can take that out into an external realm or have it appear as a balance sheet. There are weaknesses in the ways we calculate balance sheets at the moment, which is that the cost, for instance of recycling a product after it's been made, are not accounted for, and there are mechanisms that we could improve in that area, but fundamentally, it's a cultural change, to where we recognize that the purpose of what we are doing is to serve life. It's not to serve money.

Nicholas: In your opening remarks you said that the shift in Capitalism that you're envisioning has to start on the inside; that it's something that will happen through individuals transforming themselves to a higher plane of being. Obviously, we have to live in the world that exists, with the people that exist. How are you going to bring along all those people that don't think like you?

Jon: I don't think I can. I don't think it's about me bringing people along. It is about each of us finding the place to step back, and really look at our life as it is. There's a lot of hamster-on-a-wheel behavior at the moment, and a lot of that is driven by some fairly deep inner sense of lack and fear that there won't be enough, which can lead to greed, which forces us to take everything we can get right now, to protect us against the fear that there won't be enough, and it leads into power-based behavior.

There are all sorts of things involved where people lose a sense of their relationship with themselves and with others. I can't force anybody to go into that area. All I can do is offer the perception that actually, if we start to reflect, if we start to step back and ask what do we really want out of life and what are our real priorities, then that can take us into a place where we look more to what we're trying to create with each other, with our communities, with the quality of our material life in balance with the quality of all the other aspects of our health, and our stress, and our relationships with others, and our expression of our creativity, all those things that people fundamentally want to do. I include creativity. I include stuff like sport. Lots of people want to participate in sport.

Melanie: Jon, I really agree with what you're saying about valuing things holistically, and I can get excited about that, and I like the way you're including the Earth as a participant, but I'm thinking, "What can I do?" I'm sitting here looking at you thinking, "Yes," but apart from living within my means, I don't know what else I can actually do to support this evolution of capitalism.

Jon: Change is a mindset, it's not a kind of prescription. I could tell you to go out and recycle, but that's already there. It's more the inner space that people are operating from which allows them to put their attention into, "What really matters to me? What is life actually about?"

Melanie: I feel I am already in that space though, Jon, I really do, and I want to do more. I want to see your bigger picture; I don't know how it's going to all come together.

Jon: A lot of this is about bringing the relationships, the decisions about what happens, back locally. Campaigning for things that you can see locally that could be done. That's actually easier to influence than big government is. So, whatever you can see to do, it's almost like if there's a campaign to improve a hospital in your area, or something that supports a local sports facility, it's just about getting out and giving the attention and the time to doing those things, and putting the energy into the quality of life rather than the amount of financial creation we can do.

Nicholas: Part six of your Manifesto deals with personal relationships. What would be a healthy place to live in, in this respect?

Jon: It would be a mixture of some old values, which would be about service, and duty, and responsibility, and all the things which are a bedrock of a healthy way of living, and of something which has to do with a shift in our self-esteem and our valuing of others, where what we aspire to, what we value; the people we make to be our heroes are the ones out there making something happen for the benefit of others, the ones who are, yes, heroes and celebrities in their own lives, and their own local cultures.

Nicholas: What is there that's really attractive about personal financial accountability and a more healthy culture around money?

Jon: What's attractive is that the outcomes are a happier world, a world where people start to rebuild relationships, because the culture has become very alienated, there's a lot of people who live very solitary lives, even when they're with other people. Rebuilding that sense of community, and the physicality, the actuality of community, which is also part of that sense of doing stuff locally. And remembering the reason we're here, if there is any reason, is to have some happy quality-filled healthy life. And so, if the things that we're doing don't deliver that, then let's not do them, and if there's something else which does deliver that, let's do those instead, and out of that comes the notion of a world that is care first, instead of money first.

Money was invented to serve us. We seem to have completely lost sight of the fact that it's a tool, and it has somehow become a master. We serve the money these days. Well, that's stupid, that can't be right. That's not what it's for.

Nicholas: How should it be?

Jon: It should be that we are the masters of our relationship with money; we are the masters of the systems that we create around money, so that money is there to serve our impulse towards a better quality of life.

Nicholas: Part seven of your Manifesto says that we need to learn how to place financial value on what really makes people happy. Could you expand on that?

Jon: That's quite a big subject, and I guess it starts where we've got into a place where we value the money, when actually money was not what we were born to do. What we were born to do was to be happy, and love one another, and bring up our children, and have some good times, and be creative, and make music, and play sport, and do all those things that actually turn us on. We don't have any systems for valuing that into the way we make decisions.

Something similar has happened in corporations, where there's no ability inside a corporation to place any kind of financial value on human happiness, that there's a perverse thing that happens. You can show that corporations which manage all their engaged stakeholders, like customers and suppliers, and the employees, and their surrounding community, and their responsibility to the environment, those that manage that really well, actually thrive. They make up to 10 times as much profit as the average. All this is in a great book called *Firms of Endearment*, if anybody wants to look it up.

So, doing things the right way works. It's not true that we make better business by doing what we do now. So, we need to have systems for the management of companies that ensures that they understand this, that they are in their decision-making representative of not just their shareholders, but of all the other stakeholders. We need to have financial systems that make sure that environmental damage affects directly the bottom line of a company, and doesn't just disappear into some other part of our economic accounting as a societal cost that gets picked up by taxation and putting stuff right.

We, altogether, need to shift the whole way we look at the relationship between the value of money, and the value of what life is really for. And that's an internal journey as well, because we've all got seduced into the place where both parents work, and nobody has time for the children, where I'd like to have more time for my children, and somehow my working environment doesn't support me to do that, and where somebody has to take care of those in my family, who are in need, rather than me doing it myself. There's a loss of relationship. There's a loss of all the things that make community, and happiness, and health, and the vibrancy of our national life, really work.

Nicholas: In the final part of your Manifesto, you challenge us to reassess our relationship with capital ownership, and growth. Why do we need to do that?

Jon: If you have a planet which has a steadily increasing population, and a dwindling resource supply, and more and more expensive resources, in terms of getting those out of the ground, then you can't have continual growth, it simply isn't possible. It's a train heading towards a wall.

Where the notion of growth being essential comes from, is that when we live permanently with debt money, the only place that that money can be paid back from is if you have more money in the future than you have now, and that means that people think about interest. They want more money, because you've got to pay what you've already paid for, and you've got to pay for the extra, to pay for the debt. So it seems you've got have more money in the future. That always puts us under tension, and if we can't have growth, then you have to look at another way of handling that problem.

One of the things about people having capital right now is that there is an expectation that capital, just having it, will give a return. "I'm entitled to more next year than I have now, just because I already have some." Why? There's no sense in that of, "I have part of the communal wealth pot sitting in my possession right now. There is also a responsibility for what is the value of that communal wealth pot to us all, and what must I be doing in order to make that serve us all?"

It is possible to set up interest so that you have to pay interest for owning money, as an incentive to go out and do something useful with it, to support a business that need to improve, or to be philanthropic with it, to improve the quality of other people's lives.

One of the things about money in the economy is that people think about the amount of money as if it's fixed, but the effectiveness of the economy also has to do with how fast is that going through, how fast am I giving it to you, and you're giving it to somebody else, and that's what creates business. There are some great examples from the past of how people have set up systems to make that speed happen, just by creating that form of negative interest.

Nicholas: Can you give an example of that?

Jon: Okay, so, the best known example, it was during the depression of the 1930s, in an Austrian town called Worgl, where the mayor created a local currency, and that local currency had a mechanism where you had to pay to put a stamp on that money in order to maintain its value. If you didn't put the stamp on, it would lose its value. That meant that people started getting rid of the money faster. So, they started to create more business, and in the middle of the worst depression that we've known historically, the economy of the town thrived. It grew by something like 14 fold over a period of a year, before the big government came and closed it down, but it was proved to work.

Now, that's an extreme version, we probably couldn't expect 14 times growth, but what we could expect is that if we put that element into the balance of how the economy runs, we could shift the speed at which the economy functions.

Nicholas: One of the things we're really noticing at the moment, directly, is the psychology of a recession, what happens to people when they get into a mentality of scarcity, of there not being enough, or things closing down, things getting smaller, etc., and we see how very quickly confidence collapses; people close down and stop taking risks.

The flip side to that is of course, the real psychology of the boom, with the greed cycle that goes on there. When you talk about getting away from a culture of growth, how is it possible to go down that middle line between the two, without the risk of going into a stasis, a trudging through mud, not really going anywhere?

Jon: Okay, so, one of the problems with the way we look at growth at the moment is that growth is measured purely by money, not by creating something new. We definitely need growth and we definitely need creativity, but we need growth and creativity in the sense that there is the development of something new, a new product, or there's an improvement to a process, that we're investing in the growth of something that is physical, real, and qualitative, not something which is just out of the funny money. That is where we're measuring a lot of the growth at the moment, and in reality where the effect of that form of growth is simply that it eventually translates into inflation, or into the loss of the value of your pension, so it doesn't physically work for us. There's always a pay back. There was no free lunch. It always has to be paid back from somewhere.

So, the natural incentive is that people by nature are aspirational and creative, and they will come up with new ideas, and they will want to do stuff. We don't have to force that, we simply have to make sure we don't block it and constrain it, so we make sure there's money available to support it, which is one of the things that ensuring the money is flowing will do.

When we operate our view of growth and creativity in that way, we're not buying into the bubble version that makes it just be about greed and acquisition, and all the things which have got us into this unpleasant state, where we are now. We can make it be healthy, fundamentally. It's a healthy form of expansion.

Nicholas: Jon, thank you very much indeed for a fascinating interview, sharing your manifesto with us.

Melanie: Thank you Jon.

Jon: That's my pleasure.

Transpartisan Politics

The Power of Integrating Diversity

Dr Nicholas Beecroft interviews Joseph McCormick

Joseph McCormick interviewed by Dr Nicholas Beecroft on Transpartisan Politics. In this interview Joseph describes this personal journey and shares his experience as a pioneer of Transpartisan politics in the United States. Transpartisan Politics is an approach to politics which is integral and holistic. It seeks to go beyond the old divisions of left/right, conservative/liberal, authoritarian/libertarian, nationalist/internationalist, individual/group, control/freedom, heart/mind, masculine/feminine, courage/compassion and so on. Transpartisan politics aims to include the healthy expressions of all values from survival though to human potential including all those held by those represented. It acknowledges that to live in complexity we need to integrate the best of all the strands of political belief. Joseph uses a Transpartisan toolbox which is a set of techniques and processes which enable groups of people to align around shared vision and values and to integrate their many perspectives into a powerful way forward. It shows people how to navigate conflict, deepen listening, identify common values and concerns, defuse emotional triggers, build trust, strategic questioning and inquiry skills, suspend judgement, and honor difference.

In 1998 Joseph McCormick had an impeccable political resume: a former officer in the Army Rangers, a degree in Public and Private Management from Yale, and a rising star in the conservative movement with Bob Dole and Newt Gingrich campaigning for him for Congress. By 2001 at the age of 39 he was living alone in a cabin without electricity, deeply disillusioned with the political uncivil war. By 2004 he had reentered politics with a new approach, building rather than destroying bridges. He eventually helped bring over 145 national leaders representing over seventy million Americans into multi-day retreat dialogues in search of opportunities to collaborate—Al Gore, Grover Norquist, and top leaders of MoveOn.org, Common Cause, Christian Coalition, American Legion, Meetup.com, Libertarian Party, and Green Party among others. He has extended this work to the grassroots, working primarily in Oregon and Washington to create replicable, prototypical models of a transpartisan democratic republic at the scale of a town, city, and county.

Nicholas: Joseph thank you very much for joining me on this series exploring the Future of Western Civilization. I am fascinated to meet you knowing your incredible history, your journey through American politics from Republican conservative all the way through to a transpartisan leader. I'd really love it if you were to share with anyone that doesn't know you a brief summary of what brought you along and what brought you to where you are now.

Joseph: Where I am now is something of a catalyst, I guess I would call myself, not necessarily a leader because there is something of a movement of movements that are happening but I always wasn't a uniter. I was very much a divider in that my political career started in that realm. It started in the place of hyperpolarization, a lot of hatred of enemies. I took my military and my business and my conservative tendencies which had kind of a warrior kind of aspect to them and I focused them on defeating.

I found that when I attacked, I got attacked. Over a period of time later in my political career then I suffered the results of these abuses that I had done to others were done to me and so I reflected, I stepped away from it all and I reflected for a couple of years in a deep way through the pain of the wounds that I had self-inflicted in a lot of ways through relationships and mistrust.

Then I decided to go back into politics in 2003-2004 figuring it out practically, not idealistically or ideally but practically. How do we reunite America? That was the model that I was using. How do you reunite these polarities and I have come to find out in doing the work for eight years now, it's really applicable within organizations. It's applicable within any political system.

Nicholas: Some of the people reading wouldn't necessarily have heard of transpartisan politics. Would you mind defining it?

Joseph: It is a way of engaging in politics that moves beyond traditional polarities. It seeks to integrate all points of view; the left, right, center; powerful and powerless; those who are insiders and those who are outsiders, using models of organizational development and alternative dispute resolution; essentially dialogue processes where people sit together as equals. You have decision makers sitting as equals with people that tend to be on the outside of most political decisions.

When you build those types of groups, then you generate a collective intelligence which can deal with complexity. Right now our political system is designed in a way where it's an operating system, like a computer operating system, that literally cannot deal with complexity. It can deal with simplicity, it can deal with complicated problems but when you get to complexity, it defaults in some ways which is pretty much what we're seeing at the systemic level.

Only when you have a transpartisan political process can you actually integrate enough points of view to achieve the wisdom needed to create policy solutions that work for vast majorities of people.

Nicholas: If I understand correctly, the idea is going beyond the old divisions of left and right, Republic and then Democrat, Conservative and Labour and also at quite a deep level you're talking about integrating masculine and feminine, minds and hearts and so on. One thing I did wonder in reading through your story was what's the difference between where you are as a transpartisan person and someone who's just a Republican that became a Liberal?

Joseph: Great question.

Nicholas: Because after all, a Liberal would say that they were pluralistic, open to different perspectives, although they aren't necessarily, but sensitive, aware, wanting to draw lots of diverse opinions in for the purpose of inclusivity and complexity. How is it that that you are different from that?

Joseph: I still feel very rooted in the conservative movement. I still feel those values very strongly and they come from my heart. They are discipline, they're responsibility, hard work, the protection of the individual, the defense of our nation. I'm a former military officer. I'm a former army ranger which has the equivalence in the British system. These are people whose identity is about protection and conservation and tradition and heritage. I was raised that way. That's who I am.

I didn't throw that away. I actually used it as a foundation to grow and then open through my own personal crisis to a whole other set of values which were nurturing and compassion and community. I hated the word community. Community meant communism. It meant that you didn't love your country. I grew up at a time when Vietnam was an issue and these hippies that didn't love their country, they were my identified enemy.

When I actually lived with hippies for a couple of years, I'm talking real tie-dyed, barefoot, dope-smoking hippies and I looked deeper at their values and I said, "Wow, these people don't care about my last name. They don't care my resumé." They want to have a relationship. They want to mutually support each other and they exchange in the most amazing ways beyond currency. In other words they had a communitarian way of life that was very deeply rooted in the heritage of our country that we have lost.

As I kind of evaluated, I said, "Wow, that's just a softer set of values" and I had a harder set. I realized there was a yin-yang there and that's more or less the dynamic that I've been seeking to kind of portray in some ways as you don't have leave your liberal label, you don't have leave your conservative label. You can become a hyphenated transpartisan until you can really become someone who values, not just puts up with but values the other points of view. Ultimately I think we're going to find out we're going to have to do that.

Nicholas: Thanks. I guess you're very familiar with, obviously very familiar with Bill Clinton and probably Tony Blair as well. As you know they had their idea of what they called their Third Way of bringing together traditional Democrats or traditional Labour party voters along with what the people that style themselves as progressives or liberals, postmodern Democrats or postmodern Labour party people. They tried to bring that together in the Third Way. Is that an example of transpartisan politics?

Joseph: That's what I would call bipartisan. Our dualistic systems which have spread more or less around the world, the us versus them systems are essentially a divide and conquer strategy. The Romans would call it *divide et imperium*, divide and conquer is a way of managing an empire. If you want to build an empire then, essentially as Machiavelli advised the Medici, you essentially keep one group fighting against the other and then the Prince can maintain control.

That's more or less the system we inherited. It's actually, if we dig deeper into the roots of our Republic, the republic, res publica is based on this divide and conquer strategy. It's the way you can manage and it's the way most empires have been managed. When I see bipartisan strategies, I essentially look behind them and I say that these are agents and I'm being very blunt here. Agents are not Principals. Principals are owners. Agents act on behalf of owners.

These are agents essentially and we have the same thing happening in this country called No Labels and that's the Republican insiders and Democrat insiders cooperating on behalf of essentially Principals who are people that stand behind our political system. When I see these then I seek to create the distinction between a bipartisan evolution of our political system and a transpartisan because transpartisan includes everybody. Not just the insiders. It creates a conversation where the insiders and the outsiders can talk together as equals.

Nicholas: I read what you were saying how you started off trying to bring together very senior leaders from Congress and were very successful in doing that. You found that that they had a lovely time and they related to each other. The hardest left opened to the hardest right. It was a great success but then they went to back their normal situation and carried on politics as usual.

I saw that your conclusion was that over time you moved to the idea of a grass roots transpartisan movement, growing it bottom-up. Could you say a bit about Seattle where you've been piloting that and how successful has that been?

Joseph: All of this has been an experiment and it's been humbling to admit that. Earlier on in this experiment I actually didn't want to say it was an experiment. I wanted to say that we have got the solution, we knew the answer but obviously we don't and I certainly don't. We began with getting leaders together and then phase two was to get the grass-roots together and phase three which we haven't ever done is leaders and grassroots. There's a trajectory there.

In other words transpartisanship will not be achieved until you have the whole system speaking to itself with respect and openness. Having been frustrated with watching leaders go back to the old game, in Seattle we started a two-year process where we got left, right and center together in rooms, people that were as different as you get; the Tea Party and Campaign for Liberty and Transition Seattle and the Interfaith Community and Dialogue.

We found the polarizing issues and we found the uniting issues and we mapped them. Essentially what we came up with through August and September of 2011, was what we're now seeing with the Occupy and Tea Party movements. Essentially we're seeing a broad level public reaction to consolidated power and that's more. We mapped our conversations. We did them on flip charts and then we typed them into the computer. Much of that is documented. We have all the documents and we mapped a process where we could sit and listen to each other.

It was amazing that the new polarity, which is something we anticipated three or four years ago, is the new polarity would be not a left-right polarity. It would be a top-down polarity. It would be based on power and that's really the one that traditionally needs to be reconciled, otherwise a society tends toward a revolution as opposed to an evolution.

Nicholas: I went along to the Occupy Wall Street's demonstrations in London to interview the people there and find out what was motivating them. What was their positive vision? I noticed that around the edge there were quite a few business people and financial types actually coming in and being welcomed. There was a quite a healthy dialogue going on behind the scenes. I put out the results of my interviews to the London Business School and to a large global network of finance people and I found that generally they weren't really interested to engage and those that were couldn't see how to evolve the financial system for the better.

It struck me that the real power would come from not having two groups, the group of demonstrators and the group of people they're demonstrating against but actually there's a real alchemy in people coming together. If you could take some of those Occupy people and their creative energies inside the banks, inside the financial institutions, there might be something magical happen there. Do you have any insights on how to catalyze that?

Joseph: Nicholas, you're unique given your background. This is a great bridge. The ability to bridge these worlds is extremely important because the financial community would become very defensive. If I had demonstrators outside my office saying that I was abusing them and society, I would get a little defensive myself. Therefore I probably would not want to engage or I would say come on to my turf. A handful of you come on to my turf where I feel safe. Again it's the notion of safety, where I feel safe and then we'll have a conversation.

Then vice versa or you all come out of your bank and come down to our public area and have a conversation. What we've been really seeking to do is create neutral spaces where it is truly safe for all points of view. This is like peace negotiation because we're getting to the point of that sharpness of polarity here in the United States where the Tea Party and the Occupy people are getting together and having conversations and they're saying we're seeing the exact same thing and this becomes populism.

Now at that point people within the higher ranks of society have the incentive to engage or suppress. There's a part of me that I used to be on the side where I didn't like those hippies. I didn't care about whatever I needed to do to cause them to go away, put them in jail, whatever you need to do to get them off the streets and out of the way and keep business as usual going. We are at an inflection point it seems to me that those strategies will not work. This is too broad scale.

This is a global phenomenon similar to the 1848 or so revolutions that spread. It is a field effect. It is deeper. This is something that's happening at a scale that cannot be communicated away by PR firms, cannot be ignored in the same way. That's what I'm seeking to do is create the conversation where we can have alternative strategies. Essentially the dialogue strategy seems to me one of the most reasonable.

Nicholas: Fear is a big factor in the way that politics works and there are many emotional triggers that people have. With massive transitions happening in world politics, finance and all kinds of other areas, if people feel fearful of losing their job or of crime or of immigration or of terrorism whatever, then there can be a tendency to shut down and may be to polarize. What do you think is required to keep people or invite people into the creative space that you're talking about even if they are feeling fearful or very angry with other groups or other opinions?

Joseph: This has been my personal journey. I was fearful and I was extremely angry. I was extremely angry at the other side and then I became very angry at the establishment as I kind of saw behind the curtain the way power really worked within, in national US politics. I saw who the agents were and who the principals were. I saw the principals were essentially people that created money and agents were people who stood on the stage but actually didn't have any real power.

I've met four Presidents of the United States and, aside from George Bush Senior, I wouldn't say any of them were principals. These were not people that impressed me as the source of power. They were agents of power and that caused me to pay deeper attention to who power holders really were. I had a lot of fear, a lot of anger. That's why I've now come after eight years doing this work, to focus on the individual's responsibility. This, from my conservative roots, is the individual's responsibility to heal that.

If I'm angry nobody wants to talk to me. They can feel it. If I'm fearful then I won't even engage because I'm scared. I think that someone's going to hurt me. I have to go within myself to work on those, the roots of that and then coming out of that, I call it the me, we, it. If I want to change the it, the big system which all the Occupy people and the Tea Party want to change the big system, we've got to start with me. Then we go to we, then we go to it.

That's the level of responsibility that I am now taking for healing my own wounds and my own insecurities and my own fears is. To be honest, I'm nine months into a deep path of withdrawing from the external engagements and doing a lot more internal work so that I can be prepared to do more of the external work.

Nicholas: What sort of practices are you doing?

Joseph: I found that I was sitting in these meetings back in Seattle for two years and there were a lot of reactivities there. I would get sucked into that reactivity and I call them "reactivists" now. We need something like reactivists anonymous. Truly I'm very serious. That's kind of what we became. We became this reactivists anonymous group where the activists from all sides were coming together and sharing their anger and doing their best that could to heal it.

I found that between meetings I began mediating. I began doing a technique that you and I share of Vipassana meditation which is really just sitting and being quiet for a long time. Then I've integrated that more and more into my life and it's been very helpful. Actually it's amazing that the Indian government send their government leaders to these meditations and when they come back then they have a deeper sense of calm, a deeper sense of the transient nature of life and therefore are less reactive to reactivists.

If we can heal the reactivity on both sides then ultimately if you take the "C" in reactivity and move it to the front and you get creativity. Ultimately that's one of the fruits where you get creative public policy. You get innovation as opposed to polarized reactivity.

Nicholas: I remember having quite a learning experience whilst having an argument with a Marxist professor a very ultra politically correct, ultra left wing Marxist professor. I'd gone to challenge him on his home ground, in his place and he tried to use his rank, his power against me. He was trying to undermine me with all sorts of social techniques. When we eventually got into a debate it was very much like a First Word War battle with full force. We both hated each other, had a massive argument and we both knew every contour of every trench because we've had those sort of arguments many times. In the end I realized I couldn't possibly win. I slumped and I said, "Well, look, if you could have all the things that you want in the world, if everything that you're saying happened, what kind of a world would that be?" and he said, "Oh that's easy. A world without racism."

I said, "I agree with you what else?" "A world without sexism." Okay. Then he ran through all his anti-isms but they were all the absence of something negative and then finally I said, "But what about the positive. What positively would there be?" He said, "A world of equality of op-portunity." I said, "Well, I agree with all of these but what would the world be like if your political vision came true?"

It was amazing. Like a windsock without any wind, he just collapsed. He just sunk away. This amazingly powerful figure that I not only hated but to which I had ascribed all this power, he just disappeared and there was no one there. He softened and opened and I realized that my job actually had been to leapfrog to the other side rather than trying to fight him and to ask a question what kind of a world would you like? The only problem was that in having spent all that time resisting him I didn't know the answer to the question myself! That set me on the journey of asking the positive question of what kind of a world would I like.

Joseph: That's actually what I've been saying but not doing for so long. I've been saying that's where we need to be and when I sat in these groups of reactionists, then I was so reactive. I could feel it within my-self, all my judgment, all my pain, all my anger. Then I couldn't get to the place of what world do we really like? Very often we would try to facili-tate the groups in that direction but if we had been wallowing in the pain for too long within the meeting we never got to the positive vision of, "Okay if you're in charge, if you're the Mayor, if you're the President, what are you going to do?"

If you were the Mayor or the President, you'd have to figure out how to deal with any situation and so often the reactivist energy couldn't trans-cend the wounding. My feeling is it that through this process we're going through on the larger scale, enough of the unwounded are stepping forward and it's amazing. In a crisis or in a difficult situation, maturity or leadership emerges.

This is a new version of leadership. This is an ambient leadership that says, "Hey, what do we want? What is the version of the future that we want that we all can align with?" Every time we went there, that's how we got the leaders. When we did these leadership retreats with major national leaders from all sides, where we aligned was where we wanted to go. We aligned on values. We aligned on vision. It's in some ways the healing or evolutionary process personally and then aligning systemically to get there.

Nicholas: One of the questions that you ask people is, "Who are we and where are we going?" I wonder if I put you on the spot, who are we and where are we today?

Joseph: The answer and I'm speaking to you and you're living in London, England, the capital of a country that we became independent from, theoretically. At that time of our independence we articulated very clearly. Some very wise men that were former English subjects articulated principles. One was unity. There is unity among humanity and that transcends that all faiths acknowledge. We're self-governing in other words we're responsible for creating our lives. We're free. In other words, we have free will.

These types of values were at the heart of the answer of who we were. It's almost like who you are as an individual and then how do we codify that into documents like a constitution that gives us an operating system. Right now we have a social contract that says we are children and there are some parents in the world that are running things right now at the global level with a global financial system.

I at first was very shy about talking about the consolidation of global financial power but now it's become so widely acknowledged that the Fed Reserve and the Bank of England and the Bank of International Settlements in Basel, Switzerland are essentially the parents of the world. The people that attend those meetings and they do the governing, they're following a social contract. The rest of the people in the world are sitting down on their butts on Wall Street complaining as children.

That's essentially who we are right now. We're in this social contract that says, "We're children. We're all divided and we're waiting for the parents to tell us what to do." The vision that I have is the evolution of that res publica which is the pyramid model where a handful of people at the top dictate to the rest to an integration of a circle and a triangle where you bring in the emotional intelligence, you bring in the heart intelligence. Essentially that sounds like a soft and wishy-washy bunch of liberal talk but Conservatives have a heart too.

All soldiers have heart. All soldiers fight from the heart. Great sports people fight from the heart. It's called devotion. It's called courage, courage. I don't speak French but it's a French word. When you bring that quality into our systems you don't get command or control. You don't get domination. You don't get abuse whether it's from a banker in Switzerland or London or New York or whether it's a foreman on a construction crew that's abusing his power over four other Mexicans.

What you get is heart intelligence, you get respect. Now that banker in Basel, Switzerland is well educated and very sophisticated and he has a lot of responsibility but if they have a heart they're also going to realize, "Wow I'm connected. I'm unified with the rest of humanity and I really ought to consider the consequences of the vast power that I have over the decisions to de-fund something or to fund something." When you factor in that factor you begin to change everything and in some ways it's the simplicity on the other side of complexity. Things become simple when you engage the head with the heart.

We're disengaged. We have systems that are heartless and my feeling is through the coming or evolving crisis, this transformation, enough people will wake up to the practical strategic use of heart intelligence. That our systems will begin to shift towards more healthy ways. It won't be necessarily the disintegration of everything we know. It will be the transformation of a corporation or a core system or a government that functions in a healthier or more reasonable way.

Nicholas: Presumably there are some examples of where this is working already, some seeds that are beginning to sprout.

Joseph: That's a good question. Where do you see organizations that have heart intelligence? For example Groupon is one of the fastest growing companies in the world. I think they're started in 2008. They have 6000 employees and they have an award for organizational democracy. They operate in a circle-triangle format. They have a CEO and they have workers that are unskilled and then they have extremely skilled professionals but they have the circle process.

It's almost like the quality circles that Ford Motor Company brought in 30 years ago. They have the process within the organization to create the links of relationship. This is the Lover energy that goes with the Warrior energy within an organization. The Lover represented by the circle and the Warrior represented by the triangle, then the abuses of power don't happen because of the rankism, because of the disparity in rank. Groupon is a great example.

Another healthcare company, one of the Fortune 400 healthcare company DaVita, just won an award for that type of internal culture. These businesses are finding that this is sustainable management to integrate the triangle and the circle, the Lover and the Warrior. It takes a little bit longer to make decisions that way. The triangle process this pyramid process is wonderful in wartime and in emergency. If you're fighting a fire you want the captain of the fire company to say, "Okay get on your trucks, move out. Do this, do that. Don't talk back."

If you're commanding an airplane and you're trying to land the airplane, you got to have one guy in charge. Believe me I trust and respect that model as a former military officer. I didn't want my sergeant saying, "Well sir what are we going to … I don't know if I agree with what you're talking about here." We're not in war or in an emergency necessarily unless we create them. Unfortunately we've created the phony global terrorist wars to create the need for the pyramid process but under alternative circumstances when you engage people, when you engage them, then it takes longer to make decisions but the quality of decisions are far higher.

Nicholas: I really like the simplicity of the triangle and the circle because as you say one of the cultural transitions is that we've come from very traditionally hierarchical societies where there's right and wrong, truth and falsehood, with God or the Queen, an authority figure or parents at the top. Then as people have gone into postmodern liberalism the world of heart, of multiple perspectives, of relativism, of sensitivity, of people sitting in a circle and sharing and so on.

One of the crucial flaws in that latter way of being is that so far people at that level of values development have not been really good at organizing themselves. They might exist in a particular group or a bunch of friends or an academic department but those values are learnt without the foundation of the traditional conservative ones and, alone, are not very good at getting things done in a practical way on a big scale.

There's a theme here. For us to get to the next level, to go beyond these old divisions, we need to somehow integrate and hold things at multiple levels comfortable with paradox don't we? For example traditional conservatives would say, we are patriotic, we love our country. It's important to have strong borders, love our flag, give support to the military etc., etc. Good strong police and so on.

The postmodern liberals would say, "Oh we don't need any of that anymore. That's all in the past. That led to wars and patriotism is racism. These borders are artificial. We should have global diverse openness," and so on. Obviously we know that left unchecked that way of being is very dangerous.

How do we comfortably sit with being global, genuinely global, fully open human beings who are equal and open to all other humans, aware of the fact that America, Britain, the Stars and Stripes, these things don't exist, they're just conscious things passing from moment to moment, be really diverse inclusive multiracial, include all previously oppressed groups and so on and be helpfully patriotic? How is it possible to do all of that in a really conscious healthy way?

Joseph: Nick if I had the answer then ... sometimes admitting I don't know the answer is the way to have the answer to come. I don't know. I know within myself that patriotism has been my deepest dearest value and the love of my country the love of this place it truly has been love. I was born in Marlborough, Massachusetts which was on the route of

Paul Revere and this is where our revolution started. I walked the battlefields of the Civil War and I went to school in a school where we literally recited the names of the Civil War dead. They had died over a hundred years before me.

That connection with the heritage is real, the connection to place I think everybody has that. I've lived in Europe for a while and people in Hungary have that deep connection to their place. Obviously Britons do as well and Indians, everybody does. Russians, Chinese. The love of place is natural. I don't think that's ever going to change.

How do you in some ways not lose that identity but then be cooperative? United States and Canada did it. United States and Britain did it. It's because we have a common language and a common heritage. Now that the Internet and the global communication I think is actually unifying people. It's probably unifying people in ways that we can't even imagine or can't even describe. At some scale maybe what we're trying to describe is that the heart is waking up. I'm realizing that I am connected with people in India in ways that I didn't think I was.

I visited India this year and oh my God, it was such an amazing culture. It was so amazing to see it. It was very dysfunctional from my Western standpoint but the moment I slowed down and really watched, I saw so much that we were lacking here in the West. I saw so much peace and I saw so much acceptance. We will have an East-West integration of the inner contemplative acceptance of the natural flow of life with the will power and the direction and the desire to create and the strong value of the individual. May be over time, as Kipling says, "East meets West and West meets East."

As these two come together then maybe there is some sort of magical blend between the Buddhist and the Christian way of looking at things. I within myself can certainly relate to both of those. That's probably not exactly answering your question but that's kind of where my mind went.

Nicholas: I've read your transpartisan tool box, how you do that the process of getting people together from a huge range of different backgrounds different political perspectives and so on and how you basically draw them together in a really open-hearted, intelligent way. Obviously as a psychiatrist, I know how you do that one-to-one or how to do it with a small group in a room but, on a larger political scale, is there any way of doing that?

For example, recently I had a conversation with a couple of people who are postmodern liberal/left wing in their backgrounds, in their emotional attachments. We were discussing the subject of welfare benefits for people who are sick. I'm a doctor and I've had years of experience of dealing with people in that context. I said to them that a high percentage of those people who are receiving sickness benefits are not actually sick and unable to work. Some do it fraudulently. Some do it because they're briefly not well but they never get back to work. Some are depressed. Some lack social and personal skills. Some lack discipline. Some have tried incredibly hard but failed. I was saying there's a lot of people that the system is carrying on benefits that they shouldn't be on and it's not in their interest and it's not in the interest of the taxpayer and the health of the society. These two very rational, very intelligent, very open hearted, very warm, conscious friends of mine completely went mad and became really very aggressive and angry and just started shouting abuse about bankers and politicians. "What about rich bankers? What about their corruption of the system? What about our Members of Parliament and their expenses" and all that sort of thing. They just wouldn't address the point. They were emotionally so triggered and incapable of addressing it. How do you deal with that? Can you deal with that?

Joseph: What I'm hearing really is the reactivity of these people against the system, that they feel abused and they feel victimized. There's a victim role, may be a victim identity and they're projecting the perpetrator identity onto the bankers. I've been on side of the perpetrator very often in personal relationships and also in politics coming from the side that tended to be accused of being mean and cold hearted. "How do you mediate a victim-perpetrator dynamic?" The question I'm hearing is, "How do you transcend that?"

There's a great book called the TED, The Empowerment Dynamic. It's moving from the victim role to the creator role, moving from the perpetrator role to the challenger role. So then the creator and the challenger enter in a dynamic tension. They're in a creative tension. The banker and the welfare recipient are in a dynamic tension in an empowered triangle. Now who's the third person in the triangle? The rescuer role becomes the coach or mediator. Bill Ury calls it the Third Side.

It's a safe space to allow that conversation. We've created spaces where literally we couldn't look each other in the eye. I saw there were perpetrators that were so ashamed of their perpetration and victims so triggered by their victimhood they couldn't look each other in the eye. Over time, through a process of personal stories, value sharing, courageously going into the conflict and then going to policy, personal stories, values, politics, policy, that victim and that perpetrator ended up looking each other in the eye.

They saw each other because they heard their personal story. They observed the humanity in the other person. If you and I and others like us, Nick, can create spaces where the banker can sit with this friend of yours and discharge that charge that's there because the perpetrator also feels like a victim. The victim ends up being a perpetrator. It's a passive aggression as opposed to an active aggression. Then ultimately how do you diffuse that?

In Northern Ireland a lot of people found processes. They worked on the peace process to get this Third Side circle with the Protestants and Catholics and it's worked.

Nicholas: You wrote, "Disintegration gives us the opportunity for something new" meaning that you were observing that many of the old structures of our societies are not really working and falling apart. What might that something new be?

Joseph: It the analogous to the caterpillar and the butterfly which I'm sure you've heard. It's the caterpillar has to disintegrate almost literally. The cells go back to some sort of little soup in that chrysalis before the butterfly emerges. In this period of the chrysalis where our old institutions are beginning to disintegrate because their inability to deal with complexities.

They're an operating system that is like an old IBM 286 trying to run a society that takes Windows XP or something. We're need an upgrade of the operating system and commanding control, patriarchal res public or republics will not get us there. We're finding that out. What is the butterfly? It is to me the circle-triangle.

Franca Baroni in her book *On Governance* calls it Core Publicum. Core publicum is the evolution of res publica. It's the public heart and the moment we engage courageously from the conservative standpoint, screw the word compassion. Conservatives can't hear it but they can hear the word courage and I feel that literally in one side of my heart. Compassion is the other side of my heart. Core Publicum actually is the manifestation of institutions, banks, governments, libraries, academia, corporations, every institution that brings heart wisdom into it. That to me is the butterfly.

Then everyone is served. Everyone wins and then the victims become creators and the perpetrators become challengers. Then you have the creative upward spiral as opposed to the downward spiral that we're currently experiencing.

Nicholas: That's fantastic, really inspiring. I did say finally but, really finally, the reason I invited you to the chat really was about exploring the Future of Western Civilization. That's a very big subject but is there anything that you would have liked to have said that you haven't done?

Joseph: I identify as the member of Western Civilization and more and more I feel that the eastern and the western are informing each other literally. Our business cultures were integrating between the Eastern and Western cultures. Think of all the airplanes that are traveling between India and China and Europe and America cross-pollinating all of these different cultures and these ways of looking at the world.

Literally the brain development in the East is different from the brain in the West because we're still focused on language and analysis. In the East it's a Daoist brain. In other words the ability to integrate polarities is different. Maybe the future of Western Civilization, it's something that I would like to be in the direction of integration of the circle and the triangle. To me that's I would call a democratic republic and that to me is the sustainable form of governance.

We have had 8000 or so years of a certain model that now is disintegrating into a new model. It's a golden age, not to get too Utopian, but there is true yearning for the releasing of creative intelligence on this planet and invention and innovation in this to make life for everybody happy. You and I share that notion. Just be happy and releasing the bonds that we have placed on each other and allow ourselves to be happy. It's almost as simple as an organizing model that I try to boil down to a circle and a triangle.

Nicholas: Fantastic. Thank you so much Joseph it's been an enormous pleasure talking to you. If anyone would like to get in touch or to participate in your transpartisan alliance how would they do that?

Joseph: Transpartisan.net is the website. I have been more of a consultant than an advisor. There are many people doing what I'm talking about. Coffee Party USA is one group that's doing it. No Labels is a version that's doing kind of a bipartisan approach. The Liberty Coalition in Washington DC is another one, libertycoaliation.net., coffeepartyusa.org. I would just say it's really doing the personal work, not necessarily joining an organization because I realized that we're really seeking to catalyze the movement of movements that thinks in a different way.

Nicholas: Great. Thank you Joseph.

Joseph: Thank you Nick.

Creating Heaven on Earth

Taking Small Steps in the Right Direction

Martin Rutte interviewed by Dr Nicholas Beecroft
Martin Rutte is interviewed by Dr Nicholas Beecroft about his Project Heaven on Earth. Martin's present passion is Project Heaven on Earth which is a really simple but powerful approach to aligning people with their greatest purpose in service of their highest mission. The language "Heaven on Earth" made me feel quite uncomfortable because, to me, it sounds a bit naive, and embarrassingly religious. Martin knows that himself and was held back initially for the same reason. However he realized that we all feel very free to talk about "hell on earth" so we ought to be equally comfortable talking about "Heaven on Earth." The other advantage this phrase has, according to Martin, is that everyone knows exactly what you mean by "Heaven on Earth." It takes no explanation.

Project Heaven on Earth can be found at
http://www.projectheavenonearth.com

Nicholas: Martin, Welcome to the series exploring the Future of Western Civilization.

Martin: Thank you. Thank you for doing this.

Nicholas: My pleasure. Martin Rutte is president of Livelihood which is a management consultancy in Santa Fe, New Mexico. He is co-author of the New York Times bestseller, 'Chicken Soup for the Soul at Work' and is founder and chairman of the board of The Center For Spirituality in the Workplace at the Sobey Business School, St. Mary's University, in Halifax, Canada. Martin, you've done a huge body of work in your life and a lot of that has been around that subject of spirituality in the workplace but we agreed, actually, to focus on where your energy is going now which is into your Project Heaven on Earth. I wonder if you could introduce that and say a bit about it is, what the vision is and how it's going.

Martin: Sure. I will tell you about 15 years ago, Nicholas, I began to look at the notion of spirituality at work, not from the proselytizing point of view but really how can we bring that conversation organically into the workplace. I was doing a Keynote address here in Santa Fe and just before I was going on, I was thinking, "Well, let's suppose that every business in the world is spiritual, is that what you wanted?" I said, "No."

If we could transform business and because business is the temporal lever in the world today, then we have an opportunity to transform the world. Then this thought came to me, "Oh. Well, then what you're talking about is Heaven on Earth." I could remember seeing it and going, "You can't say that." I thought, "Well, why not? Why can't you talk about Heaven on Earth? You can certainly talk about Hell on Earth. That's an acceptable conversation so why can't we talk about the vision we have deep inside of us, for the kind of the world we want?"

That's what I mean by Heaven on Earth. These last 20 years have been an inquiry into what is Heaven on Earth for people and how do we evoke that organically and naturally from them, their own vision for the world and get them to engage in making that happen? That's the framework of what this is about.

Nicholas: Could you say a bit about how Project Heaven on Earth manifests practically? What do you do? Who are you working with?

Martin: Well, a number of things. I've done tele-seminars, workshops, keynote addresses, and in those forms, I help people discover what Heaven on Earth is for them. Not me telling them but them discovering it. I'll just give you a couple of examples of what people have done which blew me away. There's a woman who's a real estate agent in Halifax and we were having coffee one day. We were talking about Heaven on Earth and she had been on this tele-seminar of mine. We were talking about the sufferings of the world and the suffering that really, really bothered her deeply was homelessness in the world. She was a real estate agent. So I said, "What is Heaven on Earth for you, for homelessness?"

She said, "Well, obviously, a home for everyone," Then she jumped on me and she said, "Martin, you don't understand. That can't be done! I'm busy. I'm in a relationship. That takes a lot of time. I'm a real estate agent, I work 80 hours a week." I said, "Okay, Brenda. Let's put that aside for a moment. What can you do?" This little light bulb went on in her face and she's done this. She went back to her agency, called Domus Realty in Halifax, she sat her fellow agents down and she said, "Look, what I'd like to do is I want to end homelessness. I want to create a home for everyone in the world. What I'd like from you is to do that easily. So when you sell a home or an office building, would you agree to kick in $100 to a pot? We'll create that pot and we'll use it to help end homelessness."

They've raised $50,000 so far. They just launched a contest on their on their website, Domus Realty, in which they're asking people to come up with ideas to help end homelessness in Halifax and for the world. That's one example of somebody who really got Heaven on Earth and who got past the, "It's impossible. I can't do anything about it," and began to take a very, very simple step, easy step that was way beyond, in terms of what it produced for her and the world.

I think that's such an inspiring story because when we look at Heaven on Earth, when people look at Heaven on Earth, one of their first reactions, somehow is that they get overwhelmed. "It's too big. I can't do anything about it." That belief system prevents them from engaging in a simple way to do any kind of creative action. So, you have a planet of 7 billion people whose mindset is, "We can't do anything about this. We can't have a kind of world we want" and that's the mindset that we live in.

I say, "No. It does not have to be that way and you have the authority and the creativity to change it." One other example I'll give you is another woman who was concerned about violence against women. We were on the tele-seminar and she said, "Look Martin. I've gone to the police. I've gone to the government, no one's helping me." She kind of got a little hoppy and she said, "What would you do?" I said, "I don't know Susan. You could donate $5,000. You could donate a penny." She said, "What difference would a penny make?" One of the other women on the phone call said, "Wait a second. What if everybody in Lundenberg County donated a penny a day to help end violence against women?" She went, "Oh, my God."

Last October they set up a program called Making Change in which they hand out little mason jars with a picture of a woman's face half beaten and half healthy and vibrant and alive, full of light. Not only did they hand those out in her county but the next county wants them so that's going there as well. I have many other examples. When people get what Heaven on Earth is for them and get that they can actually do something about it, the creativity that emerges, Nicholas, is so powerful and just astounding to me what people come up with.

Nicholas: How is this different to the existing technologies of positive thinking, affirmations, the law of attraction or just straightforward goal setting and strategy?

Martin: I would say that at one level it's very similar and it also not so similar. I think the not similar is of most interest here. One of the issues in Heaven on Earth is a fundamental belief that we have in our culture that we cannot have Heaven on Earth. We were kicked out of the Garden of Eden. We've always had poverty. We've always had war. That is the condition of humanity so when you approach people and say I'd like you to consider something that is beyond what you believe possible, people think that you have to change your belief in order to be able to act.

In other words you have to believe you could do something in order to do it and I say, "That's fine but that only allows you to do that which you believe is possible." What if you want to do something way up here like create Heaven on Earth but that's totally impossible? You can't even enter the arena from that mindset, A. B, I'm asking you in a sense here to be responsible to make the world work. Well, that's mind boggling for people because there is for most people a line past which they're unwilling to be responsible. "I can be responsible for my work, my family, my friends, my country perhaps, but there's a line."

I'm saying, "But that line's made up. What if we dissolve the line and what if we just said I'm asking you to be responsible for the world and to play your part by taking a simple tiny little step?" One of the other things that we think is, "Alright, I want to end hunger but I'm going to have to do that tomorrow and therefore it's impossible, I can't do anything about it." But if we take one tiny little step and we have seven billion people taking one tiny little step then the story, the narrative of what it means to be a human and what it means to be humanity shifts and into that new story, new actions arise.

Nicholas: So what would it be like if a large numbers of people took this on or everyone took it on? What would the world be like?

Martin: I would ask you the same question. I think it's a wonderful question to ponder. Let's just ponder the question of what it would be like if the world was the way you wanted it. If the sufferings hunger, war, poverty were eliminated. For many people they'd never even entertain that possibility, and so I'm asking them very gently to entertain that. In the past our relationship with global or world visions has been one in which I have the answer and I'm going to impose this on you so: capitalism, scientism, in its worst form the excesses of communism, the era of dictatorships, the "I know and you don't." When we look at that world vision, that's how people hold it and they don't want that.

I'm saying Project Heaven on Earth is not about imposing something upon you but rather is about evoking something that I say already exists within you and that the majority of people in the world have enough goodness and if it were unlocked, we could have a major force in the world. I'm not saying I want to support being a people whose vision of Heaven on Earth is to kill another race of people or pollute the world or some kind of evil. Yes, that exists. For me the vast majority of the world, they are good honest decent people and I want them, us, to be in charge.

Nicholas: Martin, you've done this process of inviting people to imagine Heaven on Earth and then take it forward to many, many people and I'm wondering how does that show up? What are the different ways in which that shows up in people's lives, in their experience?

Martin: You're right Nicholas I've done it with thousands of people and after a while I began to see patterns in the answers. There are several arenas in which the answers show up. For some people, their belief structure is the way to create Heaven on Earth is internally so if I can create more Heaven on Earth in here it will show up out in the world in one of two ways: either do more of what's already there in Heaven on Earth, so better relationships, doing my art, dancing, writing. Anything that when you do it give you more of the experience of Heaven on Earth so we want to encourage that.

The other side of it is parts of your life and internal life that constrict Heaven on Earth, and so you as a psychiatrist would know that- early childhood traumas, stuff that you have to go to workshops or therapy, go talk to friends or clergy people to clean out the crapola in the way to allow more of that light of Heaven on Earth out; so that's inner.

Then there are people who say that the way you create Heaven on Earth is by looking out in the world and seeing where it's not and the major arena there is end of suffering-hunger, war, poverty, homelessness, illiteracy; that there is some suffering in the world that strikes you so deeply and is so unconscionable that that's where you want to put your energy and the belief of those people is what I call a capstone issue. We talked earlier about the real estate agent and homelessness, if she could solve that problem then all the other ones would collapse because that for her supports it. That's pretty consistent with people, if we can solve hunger the others will collapse; so that's an external.

Another external is the institutions which we also talked about earlier. Less people say that but, the language around it is "What would the institutions of society co-creating Heaven on Earth look like?" So if the purpose of Religion is to co-create Heaven on Earth what would it do and not do, the purpose of Law was to co-create Heaven on Earth, the purpose of Business and so on.

The final external one is nations, we talked earlier about Egypt in the sense that people have a vision for what Heaven on Earth would be for their country, or their regions of countries, or for all the countries of the world.

Then in between the people for whom it's inner and for whom it's outer is relationships. Relationships are the bridge between inner and outer; so relationship with yourself, with another or others or with the God or the divine. So cleaning up those relationships, whatever that means to you and getting more Heaven on Earth in that.

The final one is, 'now.' Some people say that this is Heaven on Earth and our inability or unwillingness to see it is what blocks it. By the just looking and getting which I can do in this very moment, then this is Heaven and Earth right now and we have some work to do to clean up some stuff.

Those are the four arenas, inner, outer, relationship, and now. Generally, people's answers fall into those. In a workshop a woman stood up and said, "The way you create Heaven on Earth is through love." That's very inner. Then a man stood up and said, "The way you create Heaven on Earth is by ending hunger." Then it started to argue. I said, "No, no, no but then all you get is trying to prove each other wrong and you right. Let's all support her for doing love because that's it for her and lets all support him for doing ending hunger because that's it for him."

Nicholas: Let's say if you take politics, people are often very critical of politicians. I've met quite a few politicians and I still haven't met one who wasn't very genuine in wanting to make the world a much better place but, of course, they all come from different perspectives, have different values, have different visions, different priorities, different beliefs, and the energy gets spent on the conflict between those. You could argue that all those people are trying to bring Heaven on Earth in their own way. Politics is the place where those differences bang up against one another.

Martin: There's a question underneath that, therefore ...

Nicholas: What's different about your Heaven on Earth proposal to politics or strategy in which people are trying to make the world a better place as far as they see it?

Martin: For me your question has to do with what I call the institutions of society so politics, law, government, healthcare, military, so on. When people look at an institution of society, the notion that, "I can't make a difference," arises quite strongly. In my work Nicholas, I found it easier to talk to people about creating Heaven on Earth than it is to about creating Heaven on Earth for government or law or healthcare. The beliefs that the institutions can't work or can't as I say, "Take their rightful place in helping co-create Heaven on Earth," are so strong and so entrenched that naturally your question would arise.

When we look into this particular example of politics, your example, the conflict arises and because conflict arises it disempowers us or I look at it and I see that system is disempowered. Yet, we have people who have decided to take that world on and make it work at a new level and I gave you the example. The transpartisan guy. What's his name?

Nicholas: Joseph McCormick.

Martin: Joseph McCormick. His story bears repeating now in brief. He was a right-wing Republican who ran for Congress in Georgia and during his run, he saw the vitriol that was in society in the political arena. He was so upset by it and saw how it was not conducive to, in my language, not his, a Heaven on Earth. He decided to do something about it. Now, his choice at that instant could have been, "There's nothing I could do. I will retreat and just say, 'I'm a victim of this' but he chose not to."

His choice was, "Let me do something about it," and he formed this organization called Transpartisan Alliance. I saw him at a Dialogue and Deliberation conference a few years ago with people from the left and people from the right were doing this dialogue, it was electrifying. I'd never seen anything so powerful because he got them to go under the positions, into the humanity, and look for some new solutions. There's an example of a guy who had a choice point at which he could have become a victim but he said, "No, there's got to be a way to make this work" and he went to that.

What Project Heaven on Earth does is to say to people, "At that choice point, what are you going to do?" The woman who couldn't do anything about violence against women, the woman who couldn't do anything about homelessness or his choice about not doing anything about the political system in the U.S. They didn't make that choice, they made another choice to give people the option of that choice. The conscious option for that choice, I believe will unleash incredible creativity for the good.

Nicholas: That's it. For someone listening for the first time, coming across your idea, what if they wanted to participate or run with it themselves? What would you suggest to them? How would you say to get through it?

Martin: What I've done, Nicholas, over the years is develop three very, very simple questions to get people to understand and experience what I'm talking about. The first question is I ask them, "Tell me a time when you experienced Heaven on Earth." Shall we do this now with you so people get a better example? I know we've done it on the phone before but let's do it. Imagine it's fresh in this moment.

Nicholas: Okay.

Martin: Tell me a time when you've experienced Heaven on Earth.

Nicholas: I knew you were going to do this and I was resistant to preparing. (laughs)

Martin: I didn't want you to prepare.

Nicholas: I know. Oh, dear. (Pause for contemplation) Well, I think a very basic example would be my last birthday in a really gorgeous location by a really, really lovely beach in Cornwall with my girlfriend, going for a walk along the beach. She made my birthday incredibly special; full of love, full of generosity, loads of a very, very thoughtful presents, a very, very special time.

Martin: I want to point out a couple of things. I said to you, "Tell me a time when you experience Heaven on Earth?" You gave me such a wonderful answer. I mean, I could see it, I was there. Always, when I ask that question, the experience is so alive for people and so present. They go right back to it. Notice that I didn't define what I meant by Heaven on Earth. Nor do people say to me, "What do you mean by Heaven on Earth?" What they do is what you did, which was just to answer the question which tells me there must be within you an already knowing. When I asked the question, "Tell me a time when you experienced Heaven on Earth?" you went right to it, in this case, your birthday. Point one or question one is, tell me time when you experienced Heaven on Earth? People do know that. The second question is, I'm just going to pick up a pen here, Imagine that you have a magic wand and with this magic wand you could create Heaven on Earth. What is Heaven on Earth?

Nicholas: Well, the extrapolation of that is a world of being present in exquisite, natural beauty and relationship with others with lots of love, presence and celebration of ourselves.

Martin: Very lovely.

Nicholas: I had a little resistance in saying that sort of thing. There's a resistance to saying such positive stuff, actually.

Martin: We'll look at that in a moment but let's put that aside if we may and look at what you did say. The presence, the love, the exquisite, natural beauty ... Wonderful, wonderful words that express a deep sense of your essence. I used to say that it's an essence of your soul but rather I think it's deeper than that. In my experience, Nicholas in doing workshops and talks in which I ask the second question, "Here's the magic wand and tell me a time when you experienced Heaven on Earth," people go to such an incredibly deep place so quickly.

The communication, the speaking, the energetic that comes out is so wonderful. It's so holy and I'm always moved by it. I've asked hundreds, thousands of people this. You notice that you don't say, "Well, it's got to be this and it got to ..." People are never positional about it. They're sharing a very deep, beautiful truth. Imagine a room of two or three hundred people, paired-sharing and open-sharing in the room. It's incredible. Everyone deepens, deepens, and deepens. We do know what Heaven on Earth is for us.

The answers are obviously going to be different and we could discuss it in our interview of the different arenas that people come up with but they do know. People do know what Heaven on Earth is for them. Then the third question is, "What simple, easy, concrete steps will you take in the next 24 hours to move that forward?"

Nicholas: (Pause for contemplation) The most obvious thing is to bring that presence of mind to my relationships with others.

Martin: That's lovely, so will you? Will you do it right now? (Nicholas chuckling) You are doing it right now? Thank you. Those are the three questions. Tell me a time you experienced Heaven on Earth, use the magic wand if you could have Heaven on Earth, what is Heaven on Earth for you, and tell me one or two simple, easy, concrete steps that you will take in the next 24 hours. I don't want you to be overwhelmed, I do want you to start moving forward. Those three questions get at it in such a profound way that I'm always blown away by what people say but the space that it come from is always that same space of purity and honesty and self-truth and never positionality, never wanting to impose it on you, never.

Nicholas: What's required to sustain that over time? People are busy or they might start and run into a hurdle or distraction, difficulty or whatever.

Martin: Let me come back and answer that in a second but are you interested in exploring the notion of your resistance to answering the question?

Nicholas: Okay, yes. (Nicholas laughing, hesitant)

Martin: Go ahead, because there is some resistance and it's not just in you it's in others. Let's explore. Why don't you give me what you think it is first, and then I'll give you my experience with other people?

Nicholas: (Pause for contemplation) I think there are probably multiple levels. One level is probably, a psychoanalytic level, the suppression of joy; of holding back on joy. Another might be my hippie "lala" monitor. That's my British cynicism. I suppose part of it is about being open in public. I think if you're open there's a risk of being shamed or attacked by cynical or malign people so there's a vulnerability in being open.

Martin: Excellent. That's true for you and I've heard it through very many people. We're doing this on Skype, it's going to go public. A workshop has a little more privacy but there still is some of that but in a workshop setting because many, many others are going through the same process. There's more of a safety and more of a support for you to go, "Oh. Well, he's saying that and she's saying that and he's saying that. I guess I'm not as crazy as I thought."

The other issue is that we don't in society give credence to people talking about their vision for the kind of world that they want because A, you'll be laughed at, "That's stupid. Don't you know that impossible? Who the heck do you think you are?" It's the notion of, "I want to look good," or the addiction of looking good. If we take all of that away and you could walk out of the room you're in now and there would be a person sitting there with a silver platter with everything you just talked about and the person said, "Here, take it." Would you can take it? Everyone says, "I would take it." Now, the 'lala' stuff is also interesting. I remember when I started talking about vision in Canada. When I was still living in Canada in the late 80s, I'd just come back from California. The words, 'purpose' and 'vision' were starting to arise as issues and I said, "I want to start working on vision, strategic visioning and consulting and personal development. I was with a group of people including my wife and very close colleagues. All of them said, "You can't do that. People will think you're smoking dope, that you just came back from California." Now vision is everyday language. There's no energy on it.

We're introducing a new notion that society said, "Well, I don't know, we've never done this." When you say, "Would you take it? Would you want that in a world," people always say, "Yes." That's what I'm after, that's what I want. Now, the British cynicism I also want to address. That's a national, cultural norm (laughing) because we created it. You guys have also given that to the English part of Canada. Real thanks. There's a tall poppy center, as they call it in New Zealand. That's just a cultural thing that we have to be aware of as well. Yes.

Those issues arise, roadblock kind of issues, whether they're personal or a conceptual level in society, arise when we look at a vision. The bigger the vision, the bigger the road blocks that come up. What generally people do is to say, "Well, let me get rid of this road block and then I can focus on the vision." Or, "Let me make the vision smaller; Heaven on Earth for my home as opposed to Heaven on Earth for the world. Okay. I can handle that." I'm saying, "No, no, no! I'm talking Heaven on Earth for the world. I'm talk about the kind of world that you deeply long for and that you would take if someone presented to you. I'm not telling you, you're telling you!"

Nicholas: If this were so obvious, so easy and so natural, why wouldn't people be doing it already? Why wouldn't it be the norm?

Martin: Part of which, you just answered the question yourself in a sense, with all those personal issues that came up. That those became more important than my desire for the kind of world I want, either personally or culturally, we can't do it. What this work is designed to do is to put that new conversation, that new inquiry into the world in such, hopefully, in such a grounded way that people go, "Yeah. I get this. This is what I want to do." When they get it, they're off. Most people are, anyway, but I'm not going to impose it. What I want to do is present this notion to you and if it resonates deeply with you and you want to engage, please do.

Nicholas: Some of what you're saying is coming from the human potential movement, isn't it? That ideal of growing human potential, being the best that we can, which you might find in psychotherapy or personal development or in coaching and leadership development and so on; in those forms. That tends to be quite a secular thing. Obviously, with the use of the term, 'Heaven on Earth' some of the language you're using is quite spiritual. How do those two bits come together or are they the same thing?

Martin: Whoa. That's a good question.

Nicholas: For some people, looking at it as a secular, psychological tool is one thing but if you start saying it is a religious or a spiritual thing then that will attract some and switch off others.

Martin: Some people say to me, "Don't use the word, Heaven, because it will turn people off." Yet, I have not found any other phrase similar to 'Heaven on Earth' that, when people feel safe enough to engage with it, goes as deep and as quick and unlocks such a huge potential. Is it secular? Yes, in the sense of human potential of your desire, the kind of world you want. In respect to the third question which is implementation, there's a very strong element of secularism, in terms of implementation. Is it also spiritual, yes.

For many people there is a very deep spiritual desire for this world to be why they've been sent here, what their life purpose is about. Let me look a little with you about the notion of Heaven. I think this bears some explanation. When I ask people, "Okay. We're going to talk about Heaven on Earth. Let's first look at the notion of Heaven." I asked people to put whatever their notion they have of Heaven in their palm of their hand and hold it lightly, as opposed to like this (gripping it), so we can break in and explore it with them.

When I ask people, "What is Heaven for you or where is Heaven?" Generally, the idea or the common answer they come up with is, "Heaven is the place that you go after death. Heaven is the place where God and the angels live." Underneath all of that about Heaven is not here, not now. That's a very important, assumptive underpinning for this work; that no matter what we do, we can't have it here. One of the first things I had to do was explore the notion of Heaven.

In the Oxford English dictionary, by the way thank you to England for that contribution to the world, one of my favorite books, I looked at the word 'Heaven'. We know that Heaven is a noun, the way I described it, the place where we go when we die and where God and the angels are but it's also a verb, 'to Heaven'. When I read that, my whole mind just went, "What?" i.e. we can go around Heaven-ing all day.

Nicholas: What does that mean?

Martin: Well, we can make this place our definition of Heaven. Is there a secular component here, with respect to positive thinking, to human potential and all that? Yes. Is it religious in the sense of our desire to have this be Heaven, not up there, but here? Yes. But underneath all of that, the three questions that subsume all of that because when you get it, what Heaven on Earth is for you and what simple steps you can take to get there, the distinction of is it secular, is it religious, dissolve. Never do people bring that up once they get it, never. Before, yes. I think it's valid before.

Nicholas: Great, Thank you.

Martin: Well, let me give you a couple other examples. There's a woman here in Santa Fe who heard my presentation in a workshop on Heaven on Earth and all of a sudden a light bulb went off. It was Christmas several years ago, it was November. She wrote an email to about 70 of her family members, immediate and removed, and said to them, "Tell me what Heaven on Earth is to you." Forty of them wrote back and that became her Christmas letter that year. It was so beautiful, so, so beautiful. That was one. The other one was a group in Sacramento California called Bread of Life. A very interesting, spiritual group that works in a very poor part of town and does a lot of stuff with art and spirituality.

I did a couple of workshops for them and the leader of it, Sandra Lommasson was so impressed by this that she created a 28 page manual for congregations, churches, synagogues on how they can bring Heaven on Earth in that conversation into their church work. Those are a couple other examples. A woman recently has written a poem about it. Sandra Lommasson and her group in Sacramento did a two month session in which they ask people to come and do pictures, or sculpture which I thought was brilliant, about what Heaven on Earth was for them. The imagery was very powerful.

Another one was a man and a woman that do relationship workshops and they wanted to ask the workshop, "What is Heaven on Earth for your relationship with your spouse or partner?" They were going to go dive into that. A policeman in Texas wrote a, I think it was, about a 20 page manual because I asked him what Heaven on Earth was for him and he said, "The end of crime." Which I thought was great. He wrote a 20 page manual for police officers and law enforcement people about what they could do to help end crime. There's no way, Nicholas that I could come up with these incredibly creative expressions.

What I say to people is that, "When you think of Project Heaven on Earth as metaphor, the metaphor is a piece of software. Let's suppose you go down to your local software store and buy a piece software, come home, stick it in your computer and boot it up, what will happen is it will present you with new possibilities and new opportunities and that what Project Heaven on Earth does. It says to you, it's possible to have Heaven on Earth, but then the program stops and it says, I can't do anything more until you put your unique content in and I don't know what that is; only you do. But once you put it in, then we can work with it."

Nicholas: Martin. I had a really lovely bunch of people here yesterday. We were making a film about their vision for Caring for Care Homes as we call them in Britain. In North America, you call it …

Martin: Senior's homes or senior's residences …

Nicholas: Right. Basically, their vision is to, using your language, creating a Heavenly care home and somewhere where the residents are fully alive, joyful, as free as they can possibly be, still connected with their family and the community and where the staff are really empowered. You could imagine what that's like and of course is in contrast with a hellish care home. Either a corporate hell or a socialist, bureaucratic hell where the souls of the staff and residences are crushed. Unfortunately many are like that.

How would you apply your technology to that setting? Taking a particular example. Suppose you met someone who was a junior worker in one of those places. Their job is to care for the elderly, to feed them, to clothe them, to toilet them, etc. A very, very important, valuable job which tends to be extremely low paid with low status and, often in those contexts, low power as well so they'll be so subject to a very controlling bureaucracy and often to quite dysfunctional leadership. How does someone like that, who knows what a Heavenly care home could be like, actually, make it real when they're really swimming against the tide?

Martin: Part of co-creating Heaven on Earth is to look at the hells on Earth and see if it appeals to you in terms of your work to make it a Heaven on Earth. In this particular case, if it's a hell on Earth, then we go back to the choice points before. One choice is that, 'There's nothing I could do. I'm a low man on the totem pole, I have no power here.' All of which is justifiable. Or you could say, 'I'm going to make this a Heaven on Earth. My position is irrelevant. What ones or two little things I can do to make that happen? We see it works because I did it in care homes here in Canada.

You could see the staff that have given up and you could see the staff who have chosen to make this a Heaven on Earth, in my language. I would bring the group together and I would say, "We want to talk about making this institution into a Heaven on Earth place." I would go through all their misbeliefs, all their "cants", it's not possible, it can't happen … I bring all of that up and then I ask them the three questions. Then I get them in touch with what for them, is Heaven on Earth in the world, in their lives and in this particular place.

Then I would ask the simple third question; what's one simple thing you could do to begin to make that happen. What you're doing is creating a new story. It's about us creating the new narrative and I say, Nicholas, that who you are whether it's the president of United States or the Prime Minister of Britain or a garbage man in either country, that is irrelevant. If we think it's relevant than we've given up on the capacity and potential of people to impact the world.

Remember those three women from Ireland who won the Nobel peace prize for banning land mines. What? Who the hell were they? What rank do they have? They knew nothing about it. They were housewives. They were women. They were Irish. Blah, blah, blah. Somebody forgot to tell those people and they said, "We're going to end this." They did and they won the Nobel Prize. Well, they should not have. Well, that's ridiculous, it's totally ridiculous. Should Desman Tutu women win the Nobel Prize? Fine. They can as well.

If you look at this year's Nobel Peace Prize, the woman from Yemen who won the Peace prize who was shared by one woman from Liberia and one woman from Yemen. This 28 year old woman in this deeply devout Muslim country was taking on the leader that's have been there for 30 years and she wins the Nobel Prize. She says in her Nobel acceptance interview, I'm going to paraphrase, "The end of women as victims has occurred." I thought, "Oh, My God. Out of your mouth there is that new context of the new world." I do not buy that that person has no power because if I did, forget it. It's all over as far as I'm concerned.

Nicholas: Great, Thanks Martin.

Martin: You could see that makes me a little angry.

Nicholas: Yes.

Martin: Not aiming it at you but because I see the power and I see the potential and I see what's unlocking but people are at these seminars and it's mind-boggling to me.

Nicholas: That's a brilliant comeback. I don't mean to be negative but I just want to put some challenges about doing it in the real world. What about Egypt now. Say, we parachute you into Cairo ...

Martin: As a Jew? (Laughing)

Nicholas: Maybe we'll Skype you to Cairo in that case.

Martin: Better, better.

Nicholas: Yes, but just suppose you could go there safely and let's suppose it's actually a pluralistic democracy which respected people. If you invited all the different people there to answer the question, "What's Heaven on Earth for you?" You can ...

Martin: For Egypt? See, what you've done is you've moved it from the institutional realm, I just want to make this point, because this is another arena of Heaven on Earth. You've now moved it to the national level.

Nicholas: Yes. If you ask the people that get on our televisions at least, they would be people from the English speaking, Twitter using, University educated level; pluralistic, humanistic, democratic; people who would fit quite comfortably in Britain, America, or Canada. They would probably talk about exactly those things. Quite a lot of people there would have a hard nationalist, almost fascist mentality seeking an authoritarian leader, seeking very top down structures, very happy to torture people they don't like, very happy to persecute Jews…

Martin: and Christians …

Nicholas: Christians. Oh, yes. A massive persecution of Christians in Egypt is going on right now and not very well reported by the media. Anyway, then you can go meet some of the more religious ones who might say, "Yes, we want the Caliphate. We want Islamic rule, we want Sharia law. We're going to take over the whole of the West and make everyone into a sub-missive Dhimmi." You could meet some businessmen who'd say, "We just want to be able to trade. We want open borders. I want to be able to come and go and for my business to thrive." The point is you would get a lot of different Heavens on Earth in people minds. They would be radically competing amongst themselves and radically competing with what other people around them might want. How does this work out, with regard to conflicts, different opinions?

Martin: I just want to say because I think our relationship is good enough for me to say this. You'll notice in the political sphere that we mentioned earlier and now in the national sphere, the issue that arise is conflict. Correct? What can we do when conflict arise? In this particular case, two points. One is that, and I deem with respect, for you, the no-tion of conflict arising would prevent people either from answering or prevent that discussion from taking place at all.

Perhaps for you, what Heaven on Earth would be, would be an insight into how you can use conflict to help create Heaven on Earth. In the U.S. there's this whole dialogue and deliberation explosion, the National Coalition for Dialogue and Deliberation has taken exactly that issue on and there's mul-tiple kind of dialogue and deliberations, specifically around that, in the sense that if we are to make this work collectively, whatever size collectively is, we're going to have to address this issue in ways that work.

That whole arena is being addressed, right? It's emerging. Secondly, in the case of Egypt, the tensions which were suppressed under Mubarak, that you mentioned, the mercantile class, the young, the Facebook generation, the Islamists and the Salafists, the Coptic Christians and the other Arabs, and the Iranian situation as well. All of this arising now because the entire system was so suppressed for years and it's all beginning to open up now. When the opening occurs, and you would know this as a psychiatrist, a lot of that stuff begins to bubble up so I think we need to have some compassion for all of that, hold them in our prayers, and I would say for me, is offer some of these technologies that would help them come together and see that there are other possibilities.

One of the things that you don't want to have occur is that unless my tribe or my point of view wins its means death to me. They have to get over that in some way. That very endemic in the Arabic world and in other worlds as well, but they have to get over that. I didn't mean to put you down in any way, in terms of the conflict thing, but it's important to see that when people get into what Heaven on Earth is for them, the very deep issues they have about how the world could and could not work arise; we want them to arise because we want to name them, put some love and some compassion around them, and give them ways to deal with it so that they can have the kind of Heaven on Earth that they want; rather than pulling back and saying, 'I can't do this because this road block is too big.'

Nicholas: Fantastic, thank you very much. Martin, you've done some writing about this business of Heaven on Earth, because in the 3 main Abrahamic religions: Christianity, Judaism, and Islam they have a notion of it being something after death and you've been exploring that. I wonder if you could say a bit about that.

Martin: Sure, Nicholas. I was thinking several years ago, 'Have we collectively, as humanity ever experienced Heaven on Earth? Is this a new idea or did it actually ever exist before?' I said, 'Well, yes it existed in the Garden of Eden.' Now whether you think that's literally true or not true, or Biblical, or whatever, it's irrelevant at this point, but the Garden of Eden story is very important in the three Abrahamic religions. It's a very strong underpinning. I'm Jewish and I phoned a Rabbi here and I said, 'When Adam and Eve were in the Garden of Eden, they ate from the tree of the knowledge of good and evil and got kicked out?' He said,

"Yes." I said, 'So who got kicked out? Was it Adam and Eve or was it everyone? In other words, up to today?' He said, 'No, it's everyone because the Hebrew language is "Ha-Adam" the Adam and the definite article indicates the collective. I said, 'Okay, fine we've all been kicked out.' I was actually sitting right here and this question just came to me and I said, 'Does it say anywhere in the Torah, the Old Testament, that after they were kicked out they couldn't go back in again?' He said, 'I don't know, no one's ever asked that before. Let me look into it.' I said, 'Okay.' The next day he called me back and he said, 'No it doesn't.' I was sitting in this chair and I almost fell over.

I said, 'What?' He said, 'It does not say in the Torah that after they were kicked out that they could not go back in." I said, 'Oh, my God! This is enormous!' So then I began to investigate, in Hebrew, Genesis 3:23-24 where the Bible says God kicked them out and he banishes them, sent them out, or words to that effect in English. I went back to the original Hebrew because I wanted to know what the verbs were. The two verbs were different in the two verses so that was interesting to me.

The Hebrew used is vah'yihgaresh "and He drove out." The root of the verb is garash. This translates as: to chase out, drive out, expel, cast out, divorce, drive away. So I said, 'Well, is that a one way verb?' and we talked about and the Rabbi said, 'It's not.' In Orthodox Judaism assuming I'm married and I want to divorce my wife, I send her out of the home, using that word; that's the verb, 'garash'. I said, 'Yeah, but if I divorce my wife could I not remarry her, assuming that neither she nor I had remarried in the interim?' He said, 'Yes.' I said, 'So it's not a one way verb.' He said, 'No, it's not.' The other verb is vah'yishalchayhoo "and He sent him forth." It has as its root shalach, meaning to send, stretch out, extend, direct, let loose, let go, set free, to send forth.

My assumption is that they were sent out with the mission of making this world outside the Garden of Eden into the Garden of Eden. That is our job here. In Judaism it's called, 'tikkun olam' to repair the world and I was just blown away by that. Both verbs do not say that we cannot go back in; that's extremely important in Judaism.

I went into Christianity and Christianity, very clear, I asked a Nun in Canada who is a Biblical scholar. 'No, it doesn't say that.' The Christ is the way, right? The, 'I am the way, the truth, and the light. Through me…' You can through Christ return. So now I had Judaism and Christianity both saying you can return, it's possible. Then I went to Islam and Islam is interesting because Islam has the Garden of Eden story as well and Islam says that they were kicked out for a limited time. It's a very interesting phrase.

I went to an Islamic scholar and he said, 'Traditional Islam interprets that language, 'kicked out for a limited time' as implying while you're here on earth alive, you're out, but once you die you go to paradise. I went to a Sufi expert who lives here and she said, 'There's another way to interpret that. You cannot only die physically but you can die egoically. So if you die egoically you are still physically alive.' So now I have all three Abrahamic religions saying that, in fact, it is possible to go back. That is so deeply and vitally important to me because I think it under- pins, to a great extent, Western society. We've been kicked out and we can't go back in. What's the point? There's always going to be war and hunger, but if that belief is not accurate. You see what that does? It's staggering in its implication, staggering!

Nicholas: I see that, but if that hypothesis was true then Japan, China, India, Southeast Asia, pre-Christian Africa would be Heaven on Earth utopias wouldn't they? Their belief systems don't have that blocking belief.

Martin: I hired, several years ago, Nicholas, an MA and I asked him to look into several religions and to see if there was anything that sup- ported this notion of Heaven on Earth. He looked at, I think 20 religions now, all of whom do have either direct language like that or words to that effect. So, I don't know about Buddhism or Hinduism, but I'm sure that given a choice like we talked about earlier if they could have a magic wand and have Heaven on Earth, would they want hunger and pain and suffering? I don't think so.

Nicholas: Thanks very much, Martin. Anyone that is watching or listen- ing and wants to read more, could you give the contact details?

Martin: Sure. The website is www.projectheavenonearth.com. The Fa- cebook group, in which I post something 5 days a week, is also, 'Project

Heaven on Earth' There's also a new book that a friend of mine put out called, 'How to Achieve a Heaven on Earth' by, John Wade. I have the concluding chapter in that book. So, 'How to Achieve Heaven on Earth' by, John Wade. Nicholas, thank you for this series of interviews. You've had me say stuff that's been clear, It has been wonderful. I think this inquiry into the Future of Western Civilization that you're on is one that all of us are on, really.

Nicholas: Thank you very much.

Martin: Thanks.

Bonds, Fields and Intentions

Culture Catches Up with Science

Lynne McTaggart interviewed by Dr Nicholas Beecroft
Lynne McTaggart is the award-winning author of international bestselling books The Bond, The Field and The Intention Experiment. She is an internationally recognized spokesperson on the science of spirituality. In this interview with Dr Nicholas Beecroft, Lynne explores the Future of Western Civilization using many fascinating examples from her work.

If everyone took all her advice and lived in a super-connected, conscious, intentional, holistic, relational way, what would that be like? The Western World is in a crisis and that this represents a fantastic opportunity for us to renew and rebalance our culture. Lynne gives us an overview of how she sees the process we're experiencing.

Lynne McTaggart is an investigative journalist and author, and a sought-after public speaker whose talks and workshops have transformed the lives of the thousands around the world who have heard her. She is also an accomplished broadcaster, who has appeared on many national TV and radio shows, including the Oprah Winfrey and Deepak Chopra shows. The hallmark of her work is exhaustive research that produces science-based discoveries in the worlds of science, spirituality and health. She edits the monthly health journal What Doctors Don't Tell You. Lynne was also the editor of the 48-lesson partwork, Living The Field, perhaps the most definitive work yet to bridge the worlds of physics and spirituality. She was born in the USA and now lives in London, UK, with her publisher husband, Bryan, and their two children, and pet dog Ollie.

Nicholas: Welcome, Lynne.

Lynne: Thank you, Nick. It's really nice to be with you.

Nicholas: Thank you so much for agreeing to join the series on Exploring the Future of Western Civilization.

Lynne: Thank you. It's great. It's great to contribute.

Nicholas: That sounds a very grand title but actually you're a very fitting person to do that because the scope of your work is incredible and going across medicine and all the full range of society really.

Lynne: Well, that's particularly the case of my latest book *The Bond* because I really tried to focus on why we're in the mess we're in and what we have to do to fix it.

Nicholas: Well, for anyone who doesn't know Lynne, Lynne started out as a journalist and went through a personal journey through her own health issues which took her into healing and alternative types of medicine and that really opened her mind.

She realized that there was a lot more to science than that which we've been taught at school that set her on an adventure of exploring all the way from quantum physics to anthropology, psychology, and so on, and she's become over the years a spokesperson for the science of spirituality, and she's written several famous and bestselling books, *The Bond*, she led the *Intention Experiment* and also *The Field*.

Nicholas: I've heard you say that Western Civilization is in crisis, that we've got big, big problems , but you actually take it as a potential opportunity. It's a time for turning, a time for a change.

Lynne: Well, yeah, and that was what I wanted to research after I'd looked at the idea that we're all connected through a quantum energy field and that our intention is an actual something that can affect the world. That led me to realize that we are really operating according to the wrong paradigm. Our story, our scientific story, has been based on the idea of us being individualistic and competitive, and when I started looking at the crises all across the board, our ecological crisis, our economic crisis, our foreign debt crisis, our energy crisis, our food crisis, you name it crisis, everything pointed to the idea that the real central problem, the virus infecting humanity was competition and individualism.

When I looked at it further, I wanted to ask the simple question, was it supposed to be like this? Were we really meant to be this dog eat dog and competitive? That led me to look at not just physics this time, but as I say, all of those other disciplines, all the "ologies." What I concluded was, no, nature actually has designed us to share, care, and be fair and not to compete, and nature has a drive not to dominate, but for wholeness and when we are like that, when we're generous, when we're connected, when we're cooperative, we thrive and when we're not, when we compete we ultimately create crises.

It might create boom economies for a while, but ultimately, they create crises. There's a collapse. There may be a regrouping. There may be greater unfairness and then eventual collapse again, a bigger collapse, and so the end game of this mindset is the mess we're in.

Nicholas: I take it, really from what you say that you see an opportunity in this for us to rebalance and actually go forward to a better way of being.

Lynne: Well, yes, a lot of people sense that it's the end of something now. We are sensing this isn't just a recession. That we've got some serious issues that signal the ending of something and a lot of people have tried to define that, but what I think and they've said it's the end of capitalism as we know it. It's the end of our dependence on foreign oil. It's the end of food because it's the end of oil. It's even maybe the beginning of the end of the world, but in my view, it's the end of a particular mindset, this idea of individualism and competitiveness and that ending is going to be the only path to our better future.

Nicholas: If we take the many suggestions that you have for how the world can be better, what would it be like, if we imagine into that?

Lynne: I wrote *The Bond* for two reasons. One was to tell a new story; the story we've been told which is very much based on the Newtonian view of the world, the Darwinian view of the world is that first of all there are separate things out there and that we're one more separate thing. The world's a very mechanistic place of separate things and that those things are in competition for whatever little is around. That comes from the versions of reality of Isaac Newton and Charles Darwin who were brilliant in their day but we have to recognize that science is an unfolding story. It's not a finite single entity for all time. It's constantly changing and revising itself and we're now realizing that those views are really outmoded, it's not really what we're like.

What I had to look at was not only the new story but what do we have to do to recover this sense of connection? Nature created us to feel the need to belong, to feel as good about giving as eating or having sex. We even have an "It's not fair" button in the brain that goes off if we're giving too little or we take too much.

Nature has designed us to connect in every way and we're happier, healthier, and more productive when we do, in every regard, business, educational models, etcetera, but here's the problem, we've all been imbued since the time we were tiny here in the West with a sense of individualism. We've been brought up on individualism. It's our mother's milk and we've been shown from the time we're little, we've been encouraged to be individual. Do you want the red pen or the blue pen? Do you want to watch *SpongeBob Squarepants* or *Bob the Builder*? It's also emphasized that we must compete from the time were little kids in school. Everything is all about competition and being first and so that is really by now totally programmed into us. To get rid of that in the programming, we've got to wipe the hard drive clean.

I felt there were four basic elements here that are important:

One, we have to learn to see much more holistically. See the whole and not just, "What's in it for me?"

Two, we have to relate in wholeness. We have to learn a different way of relating that's not adversarial because that's really what we do. Competition is the engine of everything, not only education and business but our relationships.

Three, we have to have a larger version of what "we" is. Right now, it's basically us against them and we have to understand that we need to replace that whole Adam Smith model of, "We do best for society by looking out for number one" with the idea that was proposed by a guy called John Nash, the famous mathematician, who says, "Our best response is to do what's good for us and the group." We have to have a larger version of what "we" is and not us versus them but us plus them.

Nicholas: I want to ask you about our welfare system. At the moment, say in Britain, we've got a welfare system which is excellent in many ways but it does trap a lot of people in dependency and it's not a very empowering system that helps people to grow or to come out of it. It's also very unfair for those people just a little bit beyond who work very, very hard and see others around them not working but getting things for free. How would you use the principles that you're talking about to make the welfare system fair for everybody and effective?

Lynne: That's a brilliant question. First of all, we have to understand that fairness is a real cornerstone of a connected society. When things are unfair, it undermines not only democracy, it undermines humanity.

Fairness is really essential. It's one of those real building blocks of connection and there's unfairness in a lot of ways. We're probably at our most unfair in modern times in the UK. What scientists who've studied unfair societies show is that when things are unfair and that means there's not just desserts, just reward for just effort, then everybody suffers, rich and poor.

At the moment, we've got a situation where we've got this elite who are making far more than they ought to be and that's unfair, compared to the rest of society. They're disproportionately paid and, of course, they're mainly in the financial sector. Then you've got people on the other end of the scale who are absolutely able bodied and able to work and have gone through a whole generation of saying, "Well, actually, it's better for me not to work. I make more money if I don't work." As you say, for those people who are just working stiffs who are out there working, that feels equally unfair and that angers us and it undermines our society.

A key element of creating a fairer bonded society is to create fairness and I felt so passionate about this, I created a Fairness Campaign on thebond.net which has ten Fairness Principles and that talks about not supporting anything that is unfair, top or bottom.

To get to your question, what I would do with the welfare state is severely cut it back to anybody who is able bodied. Now, anybody who is able bodied must work. If there's a situation where people who truly can't get a job then I would create situations where there are infrastructure jobs. The point is nobody but that core group of people who cannot work, people who are either handicapped, old, ill or a certain percentage of single mothers get government handouts and everybody else has to work in some way for it.

Now there are plenty of things that we need to do, rather than just giving people money. Make them earn it, even if it's state money. If they can't get a job, they can fix the roads. They can fix old people's homes. They can help build more houses. They can do all sorts of things so that becomes contributory and it becomes fair.

Nicholas: How would you advise a politician who wanted to do that to sell it to the voters because that would require an awful lot of people to change their behaviors and challenge a lot of entitlement mentality?

Lynne: There would be but there are more people out there who are middle class who are working hard and are extremely upset about this and I think they would vote for it tremendously because they would see it's not as if you're telling people to be homeless. I've known plenty of people who are single people living in five bedroom houses because it was part of their family, it was a council house and no one has picked up on it. Now that's unfair. It's pushing out another family that could use it.

I think most people would agree this is fair and just apply those Fairness Principles and also you'd have an awful lot more done in the country if, instead of just handing people money, you'd have to work for it. So you see from that safety net, it's not like somebody has to pitch a tent if they're out of work and they don't have anybody to look after them but they have to work for it and I think instilling that whole idea that if we're going to recreate a fair society, it is patently unfair that some people have to work and others don't.

Nicholas: Thank you. The way that we do healthcare is really out of balance and a lot of people's experience with hospitals is that they're very technical, not very compassionate and not very healing; that's as a patient experience. From the staff's point of view, it's a very common feeling that they're part of some massive bureaucracy that's run in a very top down way as if it were a machine and they were a cog in the machine.

How would you go and zing a hospital so as to make it a really healthy, vibrant place for the staff and for the patients?

Lynne: Okay, first of all I just want to say one thing, which is because I come from America, I have to applaud Britain for its universal bipartisan commitment to universal healthcare. I just think that's brilliant, and when I see the awful things that go on in my home country where millions of young children have no access to healthcare because their parents don't have insurance, it's just scandalous. It never fails to put a lump in my throat when I go to an NHS emergency room with one of my kids and they just get seen, nobody says, "What's your private insurance number?" I'm impressed by that.

What I think we have a problem with is the emphasis on the wrong set of tools because the problem I have with medicine is not the carpenter, is not the doctor, it's his tools, and his tool box is filled with just two things: drugs or surgery. His mind is filled with the incorrect information given to him by one of the most profitable industries in the world and that is the pharmaceutical industry and the pharmaceutical industry has been shown to be extraordinarily corrupt. Things are not effective and the information is hidden. Things are dangerous and the information is hidden.

They're corrupt. A lot of their research is written by public relations firms and they don't work. I always put this challenge out to people saying, besides antibiotics, name one drug out there that actually cures things and I think it's maybe cold sores, they now have something for that and that's about it. Drugs just don't work, they're too mechanistic a thing for the dynamic process and the holistic process that is the human body.

When you get right down to it, the NHS is not working so well because it's just wasting its money on junk that doesn't work. What I would like to see and I think people are talking about this because there has to be a real cut back in the monies paid into the NHS, so even the power that be are starting to look at alternative treatments. The bottom line for chronic illnesses is that modern medicine, conventional medicine as we know it does not work. It only alleviates symptoms sometimes and creates worse side effects in most cases. It never cures anything because it can't, that kind of mechanistic system can't.

On the other hand, conventional medicine is fabulous for emergency care. If I got run over tomorrow, I wouldn't want homeopathy to put me back together again. I'd want the best and brightest of modern medicine to do that with all of its high-tech magic. For me, I would have a highly integrated approach that cuts back conventional medicine only to that emergency area which it's so brilliant at and then for all the other chronic issues, for psychiatric issues, for emotional issues, I would have a giant tool box that represents a big range of alternative practices, all the ones that have been demonstrated to work and that's the thing that's totally under-appreciated.

That while there's very little evidence to show that much of medicine really works in any conventional way, there's a lot of both clinical and actual scientific evidence to demonstrate that a number of alternative treatments work for various illnesses.

Nicholas: I've heard you talk about the evidence that there is for the way that people operate like a shoal of fish or how people zing together, how they align around the superordinate goals and so on. At the Western Civilizational level, is it possible for us to create a field to kind of zing ourselves, get our confidence, and direction, and get more clarity about who we are and where we're going?

Lynne: Absolutely, I mean first of all, you said it yourself. The most important thing is to become the school of fish, to come together and the fastest way to cross over divides and to come together is this whole idea of the superordinate goal and the superordinate goal is a goal that can only be achieved by the collective efforts of everyone involved. It's a classic psychological ploy and it's been studied in psychology for many years to overcome prejudice and probably the most famous study of all time was the Robbers Cave Experiment which had two groups of 12 year old boys sent to summer camp.

The summer camp counselors were actually psychologists in disguise and they first got them in highly competitive situations and had them create separate identities for themselves and they engineered it so the boys were always neck and neck in these competitions and after a while, they didn't have to engineer anything. The boys were killing each other. They were beating each other up. They were stealing each other's prizes and they hated each other.

Then the counselors, the psychologists, then engineered a series of crises in the camp that could only be sorted out by the collective efforts of all the boys involved. So they put a truck in the ditch and the boys had to work together to get it out. They put an impediment in the water supply. The boys had to work together to get it out and lo and behold the boys started eating together. They started talking to each other. They befriended each other and by the end of the camp, they unanimously voted to ride home on the bus together.

The reason a superordinate goal like this works, something that can only be achieved by the collective efforts of everyone involved, is a very simple thing. When we work together for a common goal, the science has shown our brain waves start operating in synchrony. We do become a united field.

The second thing about it is when we work together for a common goal like Oxford rowers did, working together raises everybody's individual game. They studied them rowing alone versus rowing together and they found when they rowed together, they all had a much higher pain threshold. Even affirmations that use "we" instead of "I" have been shown to make "I"'s performance, my own performance better than using just "I" alone. It's quite remarkable the power of "we."

When you go back to the whole idea of how can we come together, well, you look at what happens in any kind of crisis. After 9/11, you know when there's a power outage in New York, big bad New York, everybody starts helping everybody else. What we need to do is design a goal that everybody can come together over and suddenly those differences disappear. A simple goal.

Nicholas: I'm guessing though that those have to come by crisis, don't they? You could say we've got, you know, a desire that everyone should be well educated, safe and be housed and healthy and so on, whereas, actually, we tend to stick to what we're doing unless we're very uncomfortable. Do we have to wait for a crisis to force us to change?

Lynne: Well, we don't have to wait very long. Here we are in total economic meltdown, Europe is about to blow up. We've got a couple of more years before everything we do ecologically becomes irrevocable. We've got weird, strange weather and we've got food and water crises all over the world. I think they're pretty much here, we just have to address them just as one. Whether we start as just Britain or we start as the world, just saying, okay, well, we really have to wake up and start doing this and here's the simple thing we can all do together and it would be nothing more than that, really.

Let's take a smaller example before trying to tackle big Britain. Let's say your neighborhood or my neighborhood. I experienced this personally because we were under siege. Orange, which is a mobile phone company decided to put eight phone masts in our neighborhood and one was going to be right across from one of my daughter's bedrooms.

We were all alarmed and we got together, 12 of us, mostly a housewives brigade and we all started just automatically designating who was going to do what and we started leafleting, we started putting posters up. We've met with the Orange people. We've called our MP. We sat outside school gates and church gates, etcetera, etcetera, and this little 12 person housewives brigade ended up chasing away one of the giants of British industry. They did it twice and we got rid of them twice but, more importantly, we came together, really brilliantly. It caused this closeness in the soul of a neighborhood that we never thought we had.

That kind of coming together creates magic and most importantly, it brings people together. It doesn't matter what the goal is. It's the whole idea of working together. It's building a barn basically. In my workshops, I get people to work together designing a barn and it's amazing how people come together, starting to work over it and everybody uses their skill set to put together the plan.

Nicholas: I've heard you say that our natural state is connectedness, that we're healthier, happier, more productive when connected. That seems totally reasonable to me. It's obvious, but if that's the case, why don't we do it? Why have we got out of balance?

Lynne: Well, I think it's because we've been fed the wrong story. Not all cultures act the way we do in the West. It really starts with the story we're told about who we are. If we're stressed as individuals, if that's the story that we're individuals and it's a big tough world out there and you'd better compete from the time we're little, that's the mind view we get and it's really a mind view all about fear, lack, competition; there's not enough to go around; eat or be eaten; he who dies with the most toys wins, all of that stuff has entered our lexicon, that becomes our mantra, and I think we've been fed a certain story.

We get it from the time we're little. When I learned to read, I had a book called *Fun with Dick and Jane*, I guess it's similar to *Janet and John* over here and that book's all about the comings and goings of an individual. See Dick run, it highlights that. Now Japanese people don't get told the same thing, they get a book that reads something like this: Big brother sits with Little brother. Little brother loves Big brother. Big brother looks after Little brother, so they're taught about relationship and the interconnection between things from a very young age and indigenous cultures, even more so. They're taught that they're really not separate.

The way we're taught about how to see the world is the way our brains start working. The Japanese people have been demonstrated to actually see more. They see much more interconnection between things than we do because we see things. They see the space between. A lot of that really has to do with why are we the way we are. Because of the story we've been told. Many things write the story we live by from philosophy to religion.

But really these days, with modern man and woman, science really writes this main story we've been told and since the time of Newton and the Scientific Revolution, then the Industrial Revolution, we've been more and more taught to see the world as a big machine of individual parts and once the Industrial Revolution came along, our life was far less holistic and really dictated by the rhythms of the machine, the steam engine, modern work, the punching in of the clock. Our life became dictated not by seasons and holism but by the machine and we essentially have become a bit of a machine ourselves.

Nicholas: What do you think would make an alternative to the *Janet and John* story? What's the alternative creation story or myth?

Lynne: Well, I like that whole thing of Big brother and Little brother looking after each other and also maybe talking about the Sun that looks after you and plants feed you and you do this to them, so you get a sense that we're not just the center of the universe. We are all an interconnected whole.

Nicholas: When the tsunami hit the Indian Ocean a couple of years ago, it has become well known now that some of the Andaman tribes in the middle of the Indian Ocean actually saw it coming and they used their intuition, they used their very gentle, quiet sensing of the way the fish moved or the way the wind moved and they knew something was up. They went to high land and survived. Whereas people in Indonesia who'd been more Westernized, more in our modern way of thinking, many of them died.

Looking at a tribe like that or some of the Amazonian tribes in Western terms, they are the most primitive people on the planet but in human terms, they've got something that we've long ago lost. How do you think that we can get the best of that instinctive, intuitive knowledge and introduce it back into the West?

Lynne: Well, in my book *The Bond* and in courses that I teach, I teach just that, how to recover that and one of the most important things to look at with these native cultures who survived the tsunami was the idea that they see much more than we do. They see interconnection much more than we do but studies have shown that Western children can learn some of the tricks that they have for seeing and in just a few weeks basically.

I think there are a number of techniques that we can use to start noticing more but I think it's very important that we start learning to notice detail and interconnection and also to honor our own gut hunches and intuition because we disregard the unseen and that's also a part of seeing the whole but the real purpose for understanding and seeing all of this interconnection is not only to forecast tsunamis, although that would be very handy.

In order for us to take a much more aerial vision so that we can see that there is always more than one version of reality. It's not our way or the highway. Our way is only one way of seeing and when you develop aerial vision, you can hold supposed paradox and opposing thoughts in your head; your thoughts and somebody else's opinion and understand that that isn't necessarily conflict. There are creative ways for you both to work together to produce something much better than you had individually. It's not just about compromising what overlaps. It's about integrating and creating something better.

Nicholas: I was really interested what you said about trusting our gut instincts, because that's been a favorite topic of mine, looking at what I call organic leadership. Non-organic leadership is very much is what we do in our public sector here, where it's run in a very top down controlling way where things are reduced to spreadsheets and protocols. Somehow people know that that's not really right. They know that they ought to be trusting each other more and empowering each other more but there's a sense that you can't really trust gut instinct or you can't really trust trust itself.

Lynne: No, and as I say in *The Bond*, lack of trust kills the Bond. I'm really interested in the work of Steven Covey, Jr. in *The 7 Habits of Highly Successful People*. He has focused on the speed of trust as he calls it and it's such a brilliant concept because it says when we trust other people, everything works much, much faster. When businesses trust each other, they come to a solution much, much faster than when they have to do all of what you say.

Now it doesn't mean that you don't do due diligence but it's important to understand that trust is the real basis, not any kind of contract. Trust is the basis of anything, any connection between two people. We don't trust because once again we've been fed the story of fear and lack and competition and if we understand that really coming together is what we're meant to do, if we change our perspective on what a relationship is for and we put ourselves as a vehicle of service to the relationship, suddenly things start changing.

Also if we start sharing deeply with each other instead of holding back the way we always are, then again magic happens, where people unfold. Even the most ardent foes come together.

Nicholas: Well, I'm with you on that. When I say things like that, one of the challenges that comes back is, "That's all very nice but the reality is that we have to be able to prove to the auditors, to our bosses or prove to the Minister that we're doing things right and there's a massive fear that if we allow to be a self-organizing system and really trust people to follow their vision and values, in line with their purpose, what if it goes wrong? I'm going to get in trouble for it and I won't be supported."

Lynne: Sure, there's nothing to say that you mustn't put things down on paper but that's very different from the kind of distrust that we have right now threaded through our society, because it's based on the whole idea of this, the real cancer in our society is the idea that winning equals winning over somebody else and that is totally it on a stick.

People say to me all the time, "Oh, well, you're arguing against individualism, what about individual achievement? Don't we have to be individuals to invent a better mousetrap? Isn't this going to mean we redistribute everything to the people who didn't do all of this work? How do you invent anything if you're not individual?"

Nothing I'm saying is arguing against individual achievement, individual excellence, individual amassing of wealth, individual's possessions, no one's arguing that you must take that and scatter that away from yourself or not strive for doing the best job you can. The only thing I'm arguing against is your advantage and your individualism and your achievement at someone else's expense. That itself is anti-individual. That means that some other individual gets harmed by what you do.

When you start changing that mindset and saying, "No, it doesn't have to be I win, you lose. It can be I win and you win. It can be I win and we all win and we all do better." The scientific evidence shows over and over again that in schools where you've got A students working actually in cooperation and collaboration with C students it does not dumb down everybody it raises everybody's game including the A students. You get rid of the fear and the streaming and the competition, everybody flourishes.

In business when you work cooperatively together, there's much more innovation. Jack Canfield was telling me recently, I interviewed him, and he was saying he was working with Microsoft which everybody knows has a great climate of fear. They created little groupings, silos as he called them, of groups that were pitted against each other. Every group was in competition with every other group. I think this was for their virtual earth project, where they're trying to create a visual phonebook of everywhere on earth. This hampered innovation compared to Google where everybody was working together as a big team. People were applauded together, people were allowed to flourish and have chances to brainstorm together and everybody was applauded for a job whenever there was some sort of breakthrough or a job well done. In that atmosphere, there was a lot more innovation. We're stuck in this very outmoded idea that competition equals progress and it never does.

Nicholas: You mention spirituality. We have a spiritual challenge with multiculturalism. The native populations of the West, certainly on this side of the Atlantic, have become mostly post-Christian, secular or faintly Christian but not really and in America, they're sort of half and half, half like that and half have become more strongly religious.

Some of the incoming populations from other countries have got very, very strong traditional beliefs, strong fundamentalist beliefs. We've got an issue about how we all get along together both in terms of community cohesion and of terrorism. What is the common unifying thread of authority that runs through society?

How can I trust you and how can you trust me? What's the fundamental authority of a policeman, a teacher or a doctor? Traditionally it would go back to God or the Queen or tribe. Now we've gone to a very mixed up state in which we're partly postmodern, partly modern, partly traditional. From your observations of science and spirituality, is there a post-postmodern spirituality that transcends and includes all of them, that everyone can come together and share?

Lynne: Yes. I mean, I think the big problem is the label. We should stop calling it one label and saying it's only one thing because we're all talking about the same underlying thing. I say in my book that *The Field* isn't an argument against a religion, it's approving of any religion you want to talk about because whether you call it God, Allah, the Holy Ghost, or the Field, or we're talking about the All That Is, the Matrix, the Mother Ship, and so it really is just a perception or it's a label problem but pretty much all of us believe in a sense of awe before spirit. At least most of us, other than ardent atheists, have a certain amount of spiritual awe of something greater than ourselves and that is the sense of wholeness, the sense of All That Is, the power that is beyond us. Many people have labeled that God. Many people have anthropomorphized that and created a little guy who sits in the cloud in the sky with a long beard.

Other people have another sense of it but whatever your sense is, whether that's an anthropomorphic view, whether it's much more of a pagan view, whether it's much more of a science cum spirituality or New Age view, whatever, you're kind of all talking about the same thing. If we could simply recognize that with a bigger goal, we suddenly start connecting and realizing the connections that are between us and not the separations, the things that separate us.

Nicholas: In America that's a bit easier because President Obama and the previous Presidents will say, "God" and that encompasses a lot, and even the secular people know what he's talking about. Whereas in Britain people would cringe with horror if a politician starts using that language ...

Lynne: Although, Tony Blair liked to every so often...

Nicholas: But in secret…

Lynne: Yes.

Nicholas: What language could a leader in Britain use that we could all be comfortable with, which a Christian would be comfortable with, a Muslim or Hindu, and also someone who's a spiritual but not religious and some-one who's an atheist. Is there a common language that we can use?

Lynne: Yes, we seek the divine in all of us. We seek the spirit in all of us. I think if you use those kinds of quasi-religious but secular terms they are a big broad church, pardon the pun. I think you can talk about the All That Is, people would resonate with that, from every perspective. This is the thing, it's not that difficult to look for ways to bring people together. That's the thing that's so frustrating.

I think it's that we're looking more and more for separation because we've got this fear based mentality, this competitive based mentality and when you see the error of that story, then it becomes not too difficult to find the areas of agreement.

We have this horror of conflict and disagreement. We think, oh, my God, somebody disagrees with me, I'd better get a gun out and shoot this person. You know, a disagreement unless somebody voices it, it doesn't exist. But if it does exist, the heaven's open and so what you must do is eradicate that in any way by defending your views at all costs or by belittling the other person and just making out that the person is stupid or ill informed and not only telling that person but telling the universe. You tell the immediate world around you this person is stupid and ill informed so that you will back your own point of view because you've got to hold on to that at all costs.

If people could only understand that having a difference is not anything to be feared but something that's a creative instrument for a better outcome then you start seeing what you can both develop together, not what's just overlapping but what you synergistically create by comparing your values

Nicholas: You mentioned fear there. In Britain if I look at the Daily Mail or in America, the equivalent would be Fox News, I can agree with that and think, yes, yes, yes, that's all right, that is all happening and it's terrifying, but it's full of fear and it's very worrying and there's no solution.

We seem stuck. The equivalent on the left, the Guardian Reader will look at the Daily Mail and be horrified by the angry fearful person who's shouting and find them irritating, maybe because they don't share the same values or fears.

What would you say to a Daily Mail reader or a Fox News viewer who's stuck in that state of fear thinking, this is really bad and awful and I'm scared? What would you say to them to get them into the process of forward looking space?

Lynne: Well, I think first of all everybody responds to a crisis together. All you have to do is look at what happens when there's a flood, when there's a power outage, when there was 9/11, even when there is the anniversary of 9/11, people are all coming together and feeling suddenly something about wanting to work together, doing something together. I think the most important thing to do is to make people feel like everybody's in it, we're all in this together and in that kind of crisis people do work together.

Whenever you look at some sort of situation like that, in the main, people are quite good at jumping together and working together. Even with that Daily Mail or Fox News reader, we can say, "Look, we're all wanting to work on this together, we're all frightened and here are some of the things that we're going to do. Let's start small in our neighborhood and start doing such and such and just try it. Then when people experience that elation of all working together, it's a visceral convincer.

I think what's really important for people to understand, in my view, is that the kind of change we're talking about doesn't have to be a top down change. We always think that we have to wait for the big guys in charge to do things and we're all despairing because the big guys in charge aren't very good at talking with each other even.

Certainly in America, they can't even reach across the aisles to some-body of a different political persuasion and so things seem more and more hopeless because the big guys in charge don't have the solutions. The real message of my book *The Bond* is that it doesn't require that top-down approach.

It requires a bottom-up approach that can start with you changing you changing your world view and then changing the way you see and relate to other people and change the way you see the world and then changing the way you deal with your immediate group. By group, I mean your neighbor-hood, your workplace, your extended family, and maybe even your larger community and by creating a goal, whether it is just deciding you're going to get a group together and become a litter brigade and cleaning up litter or you're going to work together to improve the schools a little bit by of-fering your time, tithing your time a little bit or you're going to help somebody in your neighborhood who's fallen on hard times and clean up his yard and come and come and do this and come and do that for them and in the full expectation that your turn will come too or you're all going to band together and have a dinner together or a block party or a potluck dinner or something like that where you're working together for some little common goal, magic happens.

That cluster of people become a dynamic force for change because that becomes a unified little group. I call them "Bond Pods" because if you create that little group and engage it in a superordinate goal and then maybe start going into a little outreach in your community, you become a powerful force for change because one thing that I've talk about a lot in my book is how emotionally contagious we are and behaviorally con-tagious.

If you're happy, you're more likely to have happy friends, not because you self select happy people to be with but because of the natural spread of happiness along a social network. It's the same thing with neg-ative things. If you're depressed, you're more likely to depress other people and create depression in your social network. There's another thing that scientists have found which is if you do an act of generosity, some sort of pay it forward act, that will ripple four degrees down so-cial network.

Nicholas: Four?

Lynne: Four, so it'll affect your friends, your friends' friends, your friends' friends' friends and your friends' friends' friends' friends.

Nicholas: Wow.

Lynne: Of course, you can imagine that becoming this virus of good will.

Nicholas: What do you mean exactly by that? How does it trickle down?

Lynne: If you're kind, if I'm kind to you, you're more likely to be kind to John, John is more likely to be kind to Mary and Mary's more likely to be kind to Sue. I saw this in an amazing little example of Marie who was sick of the very dog eat dog office she worked in and she decided to just do one little pay it forward activity.

She decided in the afternoon every day, she said, she got her coke from the coke machine, she'd leave the change there. She'd always put too much in and she'd leave the change and she'd write a little note saying, "Your coke has been paid for, keep the spirit alive and pay it forward." This totally freaked out her office.

They created this spy network, looking around trying to find out who the Secret Santa was so Marie decided to escalate her operation and she moved up to another floor and she started leaving donuts and the same sign, "Pay it forward."

The entire office was speaking about nothing else for weeks and ultimately it became the little impetus that completely changed the culture of that office. That's all it takes because another thing that scientists have looked at when they've looked at group behavior, particularly in a behavior where people have stopped being fair and reciprocal and all that turn taking has fallen apart, all it takes are one or two little change agents like Marie to start changing the game and turning the game around and when generosity is the currency the game starts changing.

Nicholas: Thank you so much, Lynne. It's been a pleasure talking to you.

Lynne: Thank you. It's been lovely speaking to you too, and I just wanted to let you know, Nick, if anyone would like to find more about *The Bond*, they can check it out it's in many, many languages. They can check out more information on the Fairness Campaign and how to set up a Bond Pod on our website which is www.thebond.net.

Nicholas: Great.

Lynne: Thank you.

Nicholas: The others are ...

Lynne: The others are to join in the Intention Experiment, our ongoing experiment to test the power of thought to heal the world. They can come onto www.theintentionexperiment.com and for all my medical information, 21 years of a database of alternative resources and alternative ways of treating just about every illness, on what doctors don't tell you and that is www.wddty.com for What Doctors Don't Tell You, and finally for my overall website that catalogues all of my activities, it's www.lynnemctaggart.com.

Nicholas: Fantastic. Thank you, Lynne.

Lynne: Thank you so much.

Leadership with Integrity

How to be True to Yourself

Dr Mary Gentile interviewed by Dr Nicholas Beecroft
How can you effectively stand up for your values when pressured by your boss, colleagues, customers, or shareholders to do the opposite? If you already knew what was the right thing to do, how could you get it done? What kinds of stories, persuasion, strategies would you use?

Mary Gentile has spent 3 decades asking and answering this question around the world. Mary talks about how her educational program is empowering people to act on their values and to make their vision reality. She discussed how this applies in the financial crisis. She talks about the potential application to politics and how a values based approach can provide a constructive way forward in very emotionally charged conflicts. She describes how she navigates complexity-coexisting in the traditional, modern and postmodern worlds, how she deals with political correctness, absolutism and relativism. Above all, she shares her story on how individuals can be empowered to make their contribution to evolving our civilization for the better.

Mary Gentile is the Creator and Director of Giving Voice to Values Program which is taught at well over 100 business schools globally and Senior Research Scholar at Babson College in Boston. Previously Professor at Harvard Business School, consultant on management education and leadership development, she is the author of numerous books and articles, including Giving Voice to Values, how to speak your mind when you know what's right.

Nicholas: Mary welcome to the series Exploring the Future of Western Civilization.

Mary: Thank you, it's good to be here Nicholas.

Nicholas: Mary Gentile is the creator and director of Giving Voice to

Values a program which is taught over a 100 business schools on six continents around the world. She is also senior research scholar at Babson College in Boston. Previously she was professor at Harvard Business School and she's a consultant on management education, leadership development and an author of numerous books and articles, most recently and prominently Giving Voice to Values: How to Speak Your Mind When You Know What's Right. So Mary, hello.

Mary: Hello, it's good to be here Nicholas.

Nicholas: For anyone that doesn't know you and isn't familiar with your work would you give a brief introduction to Giving Voice to Values?

Mary: I'd be more than happy to do that. As you said, Giving Voice to Values or as I tend to refer to it GVV is an innovative pedagogy and curriculum and approach to thinking about, talking about, teaching about and acting on our values in the workplace. I created it with support in the beginning with my founding partners, the Yale School of Management, the Aspen Institute and it's now based and supported at Babson College in Boston. We're now at over a 150 sites where it's been piloted. We're growing rapidly.

Nicholas: Did you get to Antarctica?

Mary: No, we're on six continents but we haven't made it there as far as I know. We'll keep trying! At the heart of it, GVV is really about asking a different question when we talk about ethics in the workplace. Typically in classrooms, in education and also I think a lot of times in corporate training what we tend to ask is the question how do we figure out what is the right thing to do? We look at these kinds of ethical dilemmas and we spend a lot of time mastering both the tools from philosophy as well as rigorous logic and discussion.

That's a valuable thing because a lot of times there are some real dilemmas where it's difficult to figure out what's right. There are people who've added a lot of value in that venue but what I saw was missing was enough attention to a different question which is once you know what you think the right thing to do is, how do you get it done because a lot of times the issues that we read about in the papers and the ones that we're troubled by in terms of scandals and unethical practices in business are often situations where many of us are pretty clear about what we think the right thing to do is but we're not really sure if it's possible, if it's feasible to get the right thing done.

What we try to do with GVV is first of all is to look at examples of people who have found effective ways to enact their values in the workplace. We have the positive examples, the inspiration. Secondly we look at the methods they used. We gathered stories from people and we tried to distill what were some of the tools and some of the framings and some of the perspectives that made it more likely that people could do this. Thirdly and really importantly, we borrowed from a lot of the current behavioral psychology research and even some of the cognitive neurosciences research and positive psychology. We borrowed from that research to recognize that if you want to change behavior a lot of times it's really about practice.

What we tried to do is actually shift the pedagogy. Instead of asking people to try to analyze what it was like we said what if you thought this was right? Then we framed certain positions and then we gave them the chance to literally create scripts and action plans and to practice and to peer coach on how they might get the right thing done. Truly at the heart of it we just are asking a different question. What's been exciting to me is that the scale and speed with which this idea is being picked up and spread now even beyond business schools.

We're getting interest from Law Schools and Schools of Medicine and Schools of Engineering and Liberal Arts Schools and increasingly companies are also talking to us about how can we use this approach in our internal work?

Nicholas: What happens Mary when people take up your ideas in a company or in a particular context?

Mary: You mean what happens in terms of what they do?

Nicholas: Yes what happens to them and what happens to the strategy or the profit or the behavior?

Mary: It's really interesting. It's still a relatively new approach though I have asked that question in terms of the impact. When people ask me that question I can answer it in several different ways. We don't have long-term longitudinal empirical research asking what the impact of this so far? What we do have are several things.

The first thing we have is the fact that this curriculum was based on a lot of empirical research that had been done in other fields that I was mentioning in psychology primarily in general management and to a certain extent in cognitive neurosciences that suggests that this is an effective approach so we do have some research about that but anecdotally we're also getting some feedback around the impact.

Some faculty have done sort of pre and post surveys when they run this curriculum with their students and they've been able to chart impacts both in students confidence but also in their reported level of preparedness to act on values conflicts but I think what's made me most excited is some of the anecdotal research where faculty have come to me and said, "I taught this class and then over the summer I got a call from a student who said, at my job and this situation came up and I remembered the GVV discussion and I tried it and it worked."

One of the more personal examples of that was when I was preparing the book manuscripts and when I was preparing my most recent Harvard Business Review article and in both cases a couple of the folks who were working on the editing mentioned to me that they had really liked the approach and that they had tried it. That was really gratifying.

Nicholas: What makes you think that people don't already act on their values?

Mary: Well I guess the flippant answer to that is we look around the world and we know there are a lot of cases where there is malfeasance, malpractice and unethical behavior. Of course we don't necessarily know that all those people wanted to act on their values but I think what I hear so often when I talk to managers or when we interview students and we actually hear this in the classroom a lot of times, there's folks who will say, "This is great but my boss told me this so I don't have a choice," or, "This is great but I'm evaluated on these particular standards so I don't have a choice" or I just look at my own life and think about all the times when it's been very difficult to act on my values. The easiest thing to say is, "Oh I don't have choice." Finally I'd say when I did conduct these interviews with kind of a system of gathering names from people who would refer me to people who would refer me to people.

There were always people that someone said, "Oh this person has a good story to tell about acting on their values," and often, not always, but often when I interview these people they say, "Sure I'll tell you that story Mary but I also want to tell you about the time when I didn't act on my values." They didn't want to just pretend this was easy or pretend that they were perfect people. I think I learned as much if not more from the comparison of the stories.

Nicholas: Yes. You remember during the first half of the financial crisis in 2008 when Lehman Brothers was going down, etc? I engaged a lot of people in the London Business School network, a lot of the finance alumni around the world asking them whether this was an opportunity to shift to a higher gear in terms of values, to move towards a more values based capitalism or a more ethical conscious or full spectrum values capitalism, more in service of life as a whole?

What I found was that those people that were interested to talk, who were a small subset, a lot of them saw that that might be possible in theory but when I suggested they try that in their existing banks or hedge funds or whatever they said that that was extremely unrealistic. They said that in their minds they had two choices. Either leave, retire or go and take up being a writer, run a restaurant or something instead or stay home and be a mum or possibly theoretically set up their own bank where the owners would actually have different values but not a single person I spoke to thought it was possible to change the culture from within.

I wonder if you had those conversations with them, what would you advise them? What would you say?

126

Mary: Well as I was listening to you I had so many different reactions to what you were saying. Let me first free associate a little bit. To begin with your initial question or premise about what if the financial crisis could be seen as an opportunity? I think it's a really interesting one and in response to financial crisis and I have been a part of and I have read about a number of conversations conducted in the disciplines of economics and finance about where they were actually thinking about the things that we are teaching that either contributed to or failed to prepare us for the financial crisis.

I know there have been some seminars held by Griffith University in Brisbane. There was a convening of finance faculty and economic faculty to examine exactly that question. There is a special issue of the Journal of Business Ethics Education that talks about precisely that question. I know the Aspen Institute here in the United States conducted some conversations with some of the leading scholars in finance and economics to examine precisely that question and I've written an essay about those kinds of issues as well.

I know there are people who are looking at it. In fact just today in my email inbox there was a piece from the Financial Times; the headline was, "Is Capitalism in Crisis?" Then when you look at the various articles that they were featuring they were basically arguing both sides of what you were just describing. This is an opportunity and no, in fact, there is no opportunity here. When you get to your key question there which is how do you make any kind of change?

First of all is to recognize that if you're in an industry like finance where there are such well-established heavily entrenched scripts if you will about what is permissible, about what is important, about what our goals are, about what are the acceptable messages. I don't want to underestimate or under-claim how challenging this could be. It's hugely challenging. On the other hand I have to say that in the conversations I've conducted with people some of whom were in the finance industry, there still were people who found ways to voice another perspective.

The main advice I would give is first of all, as we do with any of the GVV scenarios, to distill what some of those prevailing scripts are that

127

let us think that there are no choices and then to unpack them and not just to unpack them but to literally practice countervailing scripts and to look at examples of people who have found ways to raise another perspective.

A lot times people feel that you have to go in and make your point and persuade people and then everything changes. In my experience that's not how it works. We're talking about huge systemic issues and so to try and deal with the systemic issue as a single individual is really not going to work. You have to address it at the systemic level. However the systemic address never happens without the actions of individuals. It's one of the issues where it's not an excuse to say it's systemic.

There still is a need and in fact there's a requirement for individuals to act but on the other hand you have to be realistic about the steps you're going to take so that you don't set it up so that you're immediately discouraged which gives you an opportunity to let yourself off the hook. It's a funny dance you have to do, a dance of optimism and also realism and you have to go back and forth with that. It's not optimism and pessimism, it's optimism and realism. In fact sometimes being realistic is the best asset of the optimist because it sort of protects you from being too easily discouraged.

Nicholas: It also is quite empowering as well because you're just one of the many butterflies in the rain forest but each one has a cumulative impact. That makes it worth doing.

Mary: Yes, that's right.

Nicholas: I've done some values work in a very authoritarian, hierarchical organization. I found two things really hit me. One was, on an individual level those people that chose to participate in looking at their values, clarifying their values, really tapping into who they're, what their vision is, what they're really passionate about, where they want to go. There was a full range of responses. Some found that really super empowering and some just found it faintly interesting and a brief self-indulgent pleasure. What I noticed was that when you talk about values people tend to think that means the nice stuff; motherhood and apple pie, world peace and love and kindness and caring and all that sort of thing. They don't mention making money or having power, having control, doing someone else down. There are these more basal values, but nevertheless important values and then also this, what I'd call shadow values in the Jungian senses they have dark side of which we may not be aware which plays out in the way that we behave. How does that play out in Giving Voice to Values?

Mary: It's a really good question and I tried to explain this a little bit in one of the early chapters in the book where I talk about values that just said the work values in itself is over determined. You can talk about ethical values, moral values which are often the ones that you were talking about earlier, compassion and justice and fairness and integrity. Then you can talk about things that I value or that you value but that aren't in themselves ethical or moral values. I like country and you like city or money is really important to me and less so to you, those kinds of values.

When I talk about Giving Voice to Values I really am focusing on ethical or moral values as they are most often defined as opposed to other things that are important to you and me, of which there are many. My sense is money is very, very important to me, there are a lot of people out there who can help teach me more and most effective ways to make it. That's not really where my focus is in this work.

My focus in this work is about enabling people to think about and act on and be effective around addressing their ethical and moral values. On the other hand it's important to know the other things that are important to me that I care about that I value because I think that, A, those may help me to anticipate the places where I'm going to pay personal tension points, but they can be strengths. If I know for example it's really important to me to be in a teaching role, I love to be able to convey information to people, it's going to tell me something about the way I'm more likely to be effective in voicing and enacting my values. Whereas if I'm somebody who I'm much more reticent, I'm much more introverted, it's really important to me to have a lot of solitude or maybe it's really important to me to feel I'm not in a confrontational role with people, I'm trying to keep everything smooth because I'm not comfortable with that otherwise, then that tells me that my approach of voicing and acting on my values is going to have to play to that characteristic.

One of the things I talk about with GVV is although the objective here is around enacting our ethical values or moral values, understanding myself in a deeper way, understanding my strengths, understanding my preferences is going to enable me to create a script and an action plan and an approach that's in alignment with who I am. I'm not going to preach to the real risk taker that he or she has to be really, really conservative and cautious. Nor am I going to preach to the person who is very cautious and conservative that they need to be more bold. Instead I'm going to help them think about how to reframe the challenges they face that can play to their strengths. Those other kinds of values are important in terms of helping me create an approach that works for me but in terms of objective, I'm really focusing on ethical and moral values.

Nicholas: Great, thanks Mary. To come to the super grandiose question of exploring the Future of Western Civilization, obviously you're in a perfect position to comment on that because not only have you been exploring Western values, American values, you've also traveled all over the world. You will have met a lot of people and discussed that. In terms of our own values evolution we've gone from tribal through to traditional through to modernist and now into postmodernist values.

There's a paradox in our culture that people in the pluralistic, relativistic and sensitive maybe politically correct sense, people would like to say, "Oh I don't want to be judgmental, and everyone has their own perspective, their own values. I have my truth, you have your truth, and it's not for me to judge and yet bizarrely at the same time there's often a fanatical hysterical judgment if you disagree with them.

I wondered what's your experience? Is there such a thing as Western values that we all share? Are there really norms or have we just become a pluralistic, relativistic mess?

Mary: It's such a great question and it relates to some of the work I was doing before I was doing Giving Voice to Values as well where I was

I designed and taught the first course at Harvard Business School on managing diversity and I wrote some books and developed a lot of cases around diversity and difference in organizational workplaces and of course this is the key issue there as well. I guess the way I tend to think about it is that on the one end of the spectrum, there are folks who would say everyone's values are different. We come from different backgrounds, different religions, different historical and political traditions. It's entirely relativistic and therefore there's really no common ground to have this conversation. That's one extreme.

The other extreme as you were just saying is you used the phrase I think hysterical. This is in the sense that I know the values that are correct and there's really no doubt about it and there's no need for a conversation there either because it's already done and set.

Both of those extremes kind of make it very difficult but not impossible to have the kind of conversation around voicing values that I'm talking about.

One of the things that I did when I first started this work is I started looking for folks who actually do research on values and folks who've done studies and folks who've done surveys. There's lots of different research in this area. I haven't conducted this research myself but I took a look at what others had done. Basically what we found is that across culture, across time, across organizational settings, there tend to be a set of values that are pretty widely shared. You might call them universally shared and the philosophers call them hypernorms.

Of course there are cultural differences, of course there are religions and political tradition differences but nevertheless there are certain high level ethical and moral values that tend to be widely shared. Now this is a good thing for addressing that relativistic objection, where you can say look there is a basis for common ground. The other thing that we learn is that these hypernorms are on an incredibly really, really, really short list.

When you come to the folks at the other end of the spectrum what you have to ask them are two things. First of the all does the issue that I'm thinking about really rise to the level of one of these widely shared really core fundamental universal kind of human values. If it doesn't it may actually be more an issue of culture or tradition or preference of style or it may not be the one where we're going to have this debate. In the old expression, pick your battles.

On the other hand if it does rise to that level, then this observation gives me an insight in terms of how I'm going to communicate because now instead of communicating and saying I'm a Muslim or I'm a Hindu or I'm a Christian or I'm a Jew and this value is fundamental and you better go along with it. Instead I'll frame it in terms of the values that we actually share. I'll say this is all about justice and justice is a value that tends to be valorized in all these traditions. It may be expressed in different ways but the value at the heart of it.

Nicholas: You can do that. You're capable of that mental shift because you operate at a high level of pluralism and can see different perspectives. How to do that if you're talking to someone who is very much in that absolutistic mindset who says, "Well I'm sorry but this is the one way or the one truth?"

Mary: This is true. Yes, that's a really key point too and I think that my response to that one I thought about a lot when I was working specifically on diversity. The way I intended to address it is, "Look if I am a manager or I'm a CEO, an executive or just a middle level manager in a corporation, I cannot require anybody to share my religion, to share my traditions in terms of those kinds of values. I can't require or expect that, a company cannot require or expect that.

What a company can require or expect is a shared commitment around certain really very limited short list of values that we pretty much all care about because we all work at the same company. We probably all pretty much care about maintaining our jobs. We probably all pretty much care about being able to work in an environment that feels safe. We probably pretty much all care about being respected in the workplace.

What I used to say to people is I can't expect the person next to me to necessarily share my views on abortion. I can expect the person next to me to contribute to a workplace that's going to be safe for everyone here or that's going to be respectable for everyone here. When you're running an organization or working within an organization it's not that you've abdicated those other values. It's simply that you understand that in this context, this particular context does not have legitimacy in requiring people to agree upon every value. It has legitimacy in requiring people to agree about a certain very short list of values that are in fact important for the functioning of this organization and all of our common good.

We used to make this distinction when we were talking about diversity about what an individual can feel legitimate in caring about, committing to, and even sharing with other people and what an organization, a business can legitimately expect or require. I did not do this work in terms of public administration, in terms of public policy and government but I think that there would have to be a similar distinction. Just as there is in the US there have been in the past. This is something that is more difficult these days given the political climate but in the past there have been very well thought of politicians who were Catholics themselves.

I remember Mario Cuomo in New York State who would say, "Look I'm a Catholic. I'm a practicing Catholic. I believe that abortion is wrong. That's how I live my life that's how I operate. When I'm operating as Governor of New York my role there is to represent all the people in this State and so I have to think about that in a broader sense and try to find the values that we can share in that public way." That's an increasingly difficult stance in the US anyway these days because of certain shifts in the political climate, but I have a feeling that it's going to shift back just because it's self-limiting.

Nicholas: Thanks Mary. I heard you talk about the way our values are often influenced by our childhood experiences and young experiences. Then you go on to say that when someone joins a company, they get enculturated with the organizational culture. I was thinking about politicians because the core of the work is about saying if you know what's right, how do you get it done? What better group to talk about than politicians because they're the people who believe they know what is right or at least how to get there. They go to Washington or to West-minster bright eyed and hopeful with all their promises and expectations and then of course it doesn't necessarily happen. I just wonder if you've tried to apply Giving Voice to Values to politicians.

Mary: To politicians. Well I'll preface by saying that first of all I have not worked with politicians and I've not even explicitly worked with schools of public policy or public administration on this. However I have had conversations with faculty who teach and work in schools of public administration and public policy who find this approach intriguing. In fact there are some folks who are even looking at ways to apply it. I'm doing some work with the University of Queensland in Australia in Brisbane.

There are some faculty there in the public sector public policy realm who are looking at the applications of this work. Last time I was there I did a session for a number of folks who were both either in city government or in other public policy roles to talk about the applications. I think it's a little tricky just as it is a little tricky in law. Law schools are starting to look at the application of GVV.

One of the things that I think is important is that a lot of what GVV at heart is about is examining the fundamental reasoning, the fundamental arguments. I call them the reasons and rationalization some of which are quite legitimate some of which are perhaps less legitimate. The fundamental reasons and rationalizations behind a certain any position and understanding them in order to be able to sort of express your values in a way that's going to heard and going to be effective. For that to happen there has to be an opportunity for a really honest exchange.

Sometimes what people would say to me is that if you're really teaching people how to voice their values persuasively and effectively, what if their values are bad values? Aren't you teaching them to be more effective as unethical people? One of the things that I usually say to that is that in a business context which is the arena for which I had developed this most of the arguments that were helping people practice to respond to are arguments for the less than ethical perspective that are already out there.

We all are already pretty practiced in all these rationalizations for why you can't act on your values. What I'm trying to do is to give people the permission, the confidence, the skill, and the practice to voice the other side but then in reality once you're out there it's going to be the free marketplace of ideas and you will not always necessarily be effective.

The problem is in the realm of the politicians I think increasingly and I'm talking here from my experience in the US so it's biased in that way, but increasingly it's difficult to even have that conversation and have that free marketplace of ideas because certain viewpoints, people are afraid to voice them. People have shut down or they just feel it's impossible.

Nicholas: I wanted to give you a very particular example of that actually. The context of this is that across Western society one of the challenges we have is that we've gone from a relatively monocultural traditional and then modernist societies and then very rapidly we've opened up to become multicultural, open to the world, open to very high levels of immigration. The specific example is that I went to an off the record conference at which the subject was immigration into the European Union and present were politicians, journalists, NGO's, academics and government officials. I'd say the large majority of the people there would be people who in that public persona would go with the politically correct position which would be to say we're pro-multiculturalism, we're pro-diversity, we believe not in open borders but pretty much no discrimination as far as immigration goes, very vigorously anti racist and so on. In America and Europe there's a kind of a traditionalist backlash saying but what about our native culture? Political correctness is making our own traditional values illegal. We're not even allowed to criticize and so on.

Specifically as far as Islamic immigration goes, the place where the absolutistic mindset meets the humanistic pluralistic relativistic one, people fear that it will be the former that takes over because the latter is incapable of judgment. The punch line is that in this environment I found, to my astonishment, genuine astonishment, that the Labour Party politicians, people from the very liberal and politically correct end of the media privately all thought that there was way too much immigration.

Specifically they were very worried about Islamic fundamentalism but they were absolutely terrified of saying so in public.

They said that if they said so they would be branded as being racists. They would be branded as being Islamophobic and therefore they just chose to keep their head down and keep parroting the old multicultural ideology. From my personal position, I believe that the choice, in their view, is between the status quo continuing and going back to some sort of traditional racist monocultural old way.

I actually believe it's possible to go forward to a space in which the different Western countries are genuinely multiracial, genuinely global, genuinely pluralistic and open to the world and at the same time having a self-confidence about shared norms, shared values, shared identity, and also having the strength to be able to say "no" or to exclude those who have intolerant beliefs or those who want to take us back to a darker past.

How would you advise someone who wants to make that transition but in an environment where if you dare speak in that area you risk being completely vilified?

Mary: Well that's a huge question. I have a lot of thoughts and reactions to what you've said. You can talk about it at the philosophical level and you can talk about it at the tactical level. Let me start with the tactical which is that there's a number of different tools that don't make it easy but they make it easier or more feasible to have that kind of conversation.

For example when I was trying to set up this kind of conversation in the US in business schools around what in our context was a highly politicized issue at the time, about racial difference for example or another one that I did a lot of talk with it when I was at Harvard Business School was around sexual orientation which was highly politicized and a difficult topic to raise.

One of the tactics that tended to work was to actually set up what I used to call pot holders. You don't have to touch the thing that's so hot.

We would set the hypotheticals where we would ask everyone, it didn't matter what your race or what your position around a particular sexual orientation issue was, to answer the question what if you were in a particular role and then ask them to talk about what was important to them.

Let me give you an example. I remember teaching a class session once when I was in Harvard Business School and it was around affirmative action which at the time in the US was hugely a political issue and a lot of students felt that affirmative action was absolutely essential in terms of creating a fair workplace. There were also a lot of students who felt that affirmative action was in itself highly unfair. It was just really, really hot in the classroom and people would go from one extreme of not wanting to speak at all to the other extreme of being hugely combative.

Finally what I did is I said, "Look." I drew a line on the board and on the one side I said, "These are people who are in favor of affirmative action" and on the other side of the board I said, "these are people who are against affirmative action. I don't care what you personally believe but I want you to tell me what you think is important to people who are in favor of affirmative action? What do you think is important to people who oppose it? What are the values that they are concerned about?"

First of all I gave them pot holders. They didn't have to say what they thought. They were putting themselves in someone else's shoes and secondly they were trying to say what is important to this person, not whether it made sense or whether it was effective but what was important to them. They generated a list and as I'm sure you can predict Nicholas, it was the same list. They all were in favor of fairness. They all were in favor of justice. They all were in favor of some form of meritocracy. It was all the same list.

Once we got that list up on the board I said, "Look what we have established here is that the values are the same. We're now arguing implementation. We're no longer arguing values. Just by taking that step back and framing it as implementation, it made it much more possible to have the conversation. It's not that people immediately agreed with each other and it's not that they shifted sides necessarily but they were able to talk and I think that's kind of what we need to do on all of these issues.

I have a colleague and a friend. He teaches at MIT but he also does a lot of program work at the Aspen Institute. One of the programs that he has helped facilitate is the program where they bring together United States Congressmen half the group is Republican and half the group is Democrat. The point of convening is not necessarily to come to a shared perspective on any policy issues. The point of convening is to enable these people to be able to talk to each other. It may seem like this is just a simple little tactic, the hypotheticals, the what if's, but I do think that's where we need to start.

Nicholas: To take that example you mentioned practical things like finding allies, for example, and also I wondered who are the best people to initiate that kind of process? Would you take the people with the most emotionally triggered responses or the most polarized responses or do you take people in the middle and move outwards?

Mary: In terms of what? I'm just trying to understand the question in terms of who would be good as an ally or who would be good to generate a group of allies?

Nicholas: Well if you were a politician who wanted to say right, in Western countries we want a global, pluralistic, democratic, multiracial, non-racist, open society and we want to be patriotic and have cohesion and some clarity around what's right and wrong, what's true and false, healthily integrating the best of all. Who would be the best people to start with? Those that are most …

Mary: I guess there's two ways I would answer that question. One way I would answer it is at the abstract or at the general level if you don't have a lot of information, maybe a place to start would be more in the center more with moderates because it's the group would be a little more forgiving in helping you have a conversation while you're learning the vocabulary, you're learning the issues, you're learning to be able to more clearly understand what's at stake what's at risk for everyone involved.

Not that they would be the only folks you would engage in the conversation but they might they might be the folks who would be more willing to participate in the learning conversation initially and to accept a certain level of "mistakes" in how people communicate with each other. The second answer I would give to that is that maybe more important to whether people are more at the extreme polarized ends of something or more on moderate end and in the center it's more the quality of mind and the generosity of spirit.

The example I would give there is that there's a nonprofit organization here in the Boston area called I think they're called Public Conversations Project, PCP, something like that. What they do is they choose very highly charged issues like abortion, issues like a Christian-Jew-Muslim conversation about religious differences. They chose very highly charged issues and they get together a group of people who may hold quite firm and even polarized views but who are in fact committed to a conversation.

That is in fact all they ask of them is they ask of them to commit to an ongoing conversation, not to take your marbles and walk away if you're not happy with what people said. Certain rules of respect in terms of how we communicate and they bring this group of people together over an extended period of time to just keep talking about it. It's not that the group necessarily comes to some shared take or that they convert each other but they in fact begin to be able to respect, understand, and talk to each other. I've seen this group profiled in various places. I've seen them do interviews where they bring in representatives.

I happened to see one where they were representatives from the abortion conversation where they had some really firm, firm, firm Catholics who just felt this was absolutely wrong and they had other folks who were dyed in the wool abortion rights folks from old, old time and they had to come to respect and understand, not necessarily agree but to be able to talk and that wasn't a matter of being polarized or moderate. It was more that they were willing to commit to the conversation. I guess I would answer it in two different ways.

Nicholas: We have been talking about Giving Voice to Values from the bottom-up. From the boss's point of view or from a leader's point of view some people would say that we've got a self-organizing living system, we want to empower everyone to live their values and tap into their energy and so on and in alignment with their goals. Others or the same people in different situations might say, "Oh hang on this isn't a democracy. We've got a job to do and people have got to pull in the same direction." Are there any risks in following the Giving Voice to Values approach from a leader's point of view? Can things go badly wrong? Can you lose control?

Mary: First of all I would say around the statement that, "This is not a democracy" and we have to pull in the same direction, I would harken back to what I was saying earlier about an organization can only legitimately ask that and expect that around a certain fairly short list of shared primary goals. That doesn't become an excuse for treating people in any way you care to. First of all you have to be realistic about how broadly you define that same direction.

The second thing I would say is that we know from much of the research that people tend to do better work, be more motivated, more creative etc. to the degree that they do feel aligned with the goals and culture of the organization where they're working. If I'm a leader, am I happy when people come to me giving voice to their values or is it going to be a thorn in my side and I think the answer is yes and yes.

We know that if people are afraid to speak truth to power, if people are afraid to tell you that the emperor has no clothes, then ultimately this is not a good thing for your organization. There's important information that you are missing. It's important information and you're going to have a problem because you don't have it. On the other hand that doesn't mean that in the near term in the short term I'm not chagrined when someone comes to my door and lays this problem on my desk.

One of the things that we do in GVV is we actually ask people to go through a process where they have to answer a set of questions in order to think about how they're going to raise issues. It's not just about speaking up. A lot of times it's really about thinking creatively about solutions or alternatives, being part of the solution as well as simply blowing a whistle on the problem. If you are the individual lower in the organization who's voicing this I think it would behove you to think about that. If you're the manager hearing this or the leader hearing this, I think that you're going to be more likely to hear this. You're going to be more comfortable with hearing it if the person who comes to you, comes to you in that constructive spirit.

If he or she has actually also thought about what's at risk for me as a leader and for the organization in dealing with this issue, a conversation between two grownups. It's not me going to mummy and daddy and asking them to fix it. Voicing values is not simply about learning to complain. It's really learning to problem solve but I do sometimes think that maybe the next book, if this book was about voicing values, should be about how to hear these messages because we'll have to prepare ourselves to hear them so that just as one of the tools for voicing values is, we call it normalization, and so reducing the emotion around us and realizing this is just a normal part of business. That's also true for the person hearing it. It's like "don't freak out don't go from zero to 100. Let's just see this as one more business challenge and we'll solve it."

Nicholas: Just to finish off Mary, as Giving Voice to Values your program takes the world by storm goes into every school, every university, every hospital, every medical school, every parliament, if we fast forward 10-20 years and people are really living it, what is that world like?

Mary: That's great. I guess I think it's a world where people feel more integrated. People feel happier to go to work even when there are challenges and problems because they understand that there's something they can do. They understand that there is possibility. I think it's a world where people are less complaining and more energized because I think people feel like it's not the world where you pick up the paper every morning and you shake your head and you go, "Oh my God! The world's going to hell in a hand basket. What is it coming too?

Instead it's the world where you pick up the paper and you see a set of challenges and opportunities that you yourself want to work on and are engaged in working on because you feel that it's possible to do so. I frankly don't think that any of these problems are made or solved by individuals. They're made and solved by groups and by systems. The only way that's going to happen is if people feel empowered, if people feel like it matters what I do and say.

If this work continues to resonate and to grow in the way that I'm so happy it began, I think more and more people will just have that … It's not that the world will … their problems will be solved, it just that the people will be engaged in feeling they have the possibility of doing so, that they can be part of that solution.

Nicholas: Thank you very much Mary, that's very inspiring.

Mary: Thanks.

Nicholas: For anyone that's listening that would like to read your book or look at website would give the address that they should go to?

Mary: Sure. The book website is simply www.givingvoicetovaluesthebook.com and the curriculum is simply www.givingvoicetovalues.org The curriculum itself is all available to educators for free and you can link from either website to the other one. Thank you for that opportunity. I should also say that the book is from Yale University Press. The paperback is coming out this month and the Spanish edition is coming out in the fall.

Nicholas: Great. Thank you Mary.

Mary: Thank you Nicholas. This has been fun.

Wisdom

Lost and Rediscovered

Professor Jim Garrison interviewed by Dr Nicholas Beecroft.
What is wisdom? How is it distinct from knowledge, truth, logic and science? Is it gut feeling, heart-brain, neurological and cognitive short cuts, tapping into electromagnetic energy, consciousness, all of that or something else? Western Science and philosophy evolved for a reason-partly because they work and improve our lives (trains, computers, medicine) and partly because they took us out of mediaeval tyranny of superstition, religious fundamentalism and serfdom. We obviously don't want to go back to that but are becoming aware that we threw out a few babies with the bathwater. How can we access and nurture our wisdom? How can we integrate it with the best of science and reason? Do they synergize or run in parallel or do they apply for different purposes? What would medicine be like if we accessed our wisdom? How do you envisage the world would be if we all learn to use our wisdom? When we drop the rigor of science and reason, there's a risk of falling back into superstitions and false beliefs which at best can be a waste of time, can be harmful. How do you discern what's true from what's wishful thinking, imaginary, delusional or manipulative?

Dr. Jim Garrison is President and Chairman of Wisdom University. He teaches several courses at Wisdom University, including the core course Wisdom and Civilization. In this interview with Nicholas Beecroft, Jim sets out his vision to restore wisdom to a central place in our way of life. He describes wisdom and its relationship to science and reason. He discusses how wisdom can be used in medicine, politics and says he believes it's essential to our survival.

Previously, he founded and served as President of the Gorbachev Foundation/USA and the State of the World Forum, both San Francisco-based nonprofit institutions created to establish a global network of leaders dedicated to creating a more sustainable global civilization. With President Gorbachev as its convening chairman, the Forum brought together leaders from around the world in a variety of disciplines to its annual and regional conferences and catalyzed the creation of several independent organizations. Dr. Garrison published his first book in 1980, The Plutonium Culture (SCM). This was followed by The Darkness of God: Theology After Hiroshima (SCM/1982); The Russian Threat: Myths and Realities (Gateway Books/1983); The New Diplomats (Resurgence Press/1984); Civilization and the Transformation of Power (Paraview Press/2000); and America As Empire: Global Leader or Rogue Power? (Barrett Koehler/2004.)

Nicholas: Welcome Jim to the series Exploring the Future of Western Civilization which is a very grand title, but that is exactly what you've spent years doing, isn't it, and trying to influence it? For anyone that doesn't know Jim, I can't really do him justice with his very prodigious career, but he is a Professor and President of the Wisdom University. He's also President of the Gorbachev Foundation in the U.S. and previously led the State of the World Forum or I think maybe you still do.

Jim: Yes.

Nicholas: The thing I want to discuss with you Jim is wisdom and how we bring that back into our lives in a credible way and how we integrate it with the way that we live? What first made you realize that we had a problem with wisdom and that we needed to re-legitimize it again?

Jim: I think there's a couple of factors in all this. One of which is that in my own personal life, it was a discovery of how the ancients actually viewed wisdom and in this regard, if anyone who listens to this has the opportunity to pick up Pierre Hadot's works "Philosophy is a Way of Life" or "What is Philosophy?" or "The Veil of Isis," they would be very well served because what Hadot points out is that we in the West, particularly since the Enlightenment have relegated the study of philosophy, the study of wisdom to very arcane academic institutions. One thinks of Wittgenstein's work in mathematical logic and so forth, but among the ancients, wisdom was a way of life. Wisdom was a way that one oriented one's existence and that was of course the origin of the term philosophy. It was someone who was a lover of wisdom. In Plato's Academy among the Epicureans, among the Stoics, etc., they gathered in community. They asked deep questions and as Socrates pointed out, at the heart of wisdom as a way of life is the disposition to live in questions rather than in answers. If you think about it in terms of basic epistemology, particularly in the West, religions are oriented around dogmatic belief. You need to believe that Jesus is your savior because if you don't you're going to go to hell, for example. In Islam, you are an either a believer or you're among the infidels. So religions are oriented around belief, faith and a certainty that's been given by a supreme God.

Science has another epistemology but, again, it's oriented around certifiable facts, just the facts ma'am, just the facts. Even though science hypothesizes and deals with different theories, it's still trying to ground itself in what is observable, measurable and knowable through the five senses. Wisdom on the other hand, lives in the questions and the great genius of Socrates was his understanding that neither dogmatic belief nor scientific certainty was sufficient to bring about that which we most deeply seek which is really personal transformation. That somehow if we're courageous enough to live in the questions in a dialogic way with either our teacher or our community that we engage as Plotinus, a third century Neoplatonist talked about in terms of, "The pursuit of wisdom is like being a sculptor. It's not about acquiring knowledge. It's about stripping away delusions and fears." So he gave the image of a sculptor looking at a block of marble. What makes a marble into a statute is that which you chip away. That the pursuit of wisdom is chipping away that which is not essentially you. That's what makes wisdom a way of life as I understand it.

Nicholas: Is wisdom our gut feeling, our heart-brain tapping into the electromagnetic space between us? Is it a cognitive shortcut? Is it universal consciousness? It's not cerebral cortex logic, so what is it?

Jim: I think it's in some ways all of the above. Wisdom like love, hope or courage are easily said, but not so easily defined so that one can discern qualities to love, but no one has defined love in an absolute sense. So anything that I would say about wisdom would be ad hoc, ultimately and temporary. In the first instance, wisdom is the capacity to see the larger context. When you think of a wise person, they're not a person who is egocentric. They're a person who understands the ebb and flow of life. They're people who get the larger picture and therefore, see themselves relative to the larger pictures, as opposed to absolute and therefore, completely egocentric.

Most babies aren't wise. They're very egocentric and they cry when they're hungry and they want immediate attention. I think there's something about maturational development toward context, rather than content that demarcates a wise person. Because they see themselves relative to the whole rather than absolute to the whole, they tend to have cultivated characteristics of humility, of compassion of sensitivity to others because they become aware of contingency. They're aware that we are fallible creatures in a very contingent world.

Then I think thirdly, a wise person understands very deeply their mortality. Remember Plato said, "That all philosophy begins with the meditation on death." That was an understanding that was foundational to all the original wisdom schools. That once one comes to terms with one's finitude, with one's mortality, then you begin to prioritize that which is important and dispense with that which is irrelevant. The meditation-if this was the last day of your life, what would you do then you have instance after instance of people that are diagnosed with some kind of terminal cancer say and they're giving three months to live. Their entire life changes and they begin to pay attention to relationships. They begin to pay attention to the here and the now. I think that's also an aspect of wisdom. I keep, for example on my desk a skull that I've had since I was 15 and it's next to a candle. Every day when I go into my study I light the candle and I look at the skull and I try to internalize, even though I forget after a few minutes that I'm a mortal man and because I'm mortal, my ultimate obligation is to love.

Nicholas: I totally agree with what you just said, so I'm not coming at you from an antagonistic perspective. What I'd like is your experience at arguing from the other direction. I'd like to put to you some of the things that people say to me to see how you deal with those challenges so I can learn from that. For example, if we put it in a very practical context, I'm a doctor. In a healthcare setting, the way a lot of medicine is done is in a very rational, intellectualized, technical, disembodied and very many brilliant things from science, but we also have thrown out the baby with the bathwater in terms of the basics like caring and healing.

Take this example. With cognitive behavior therapy, I guess you know what that is, that type of psychotherapy which is excellent, very good, but it's quite simple. Of all the therapies it's perhaps the most rational, linear, apparently measurable and simple and therefore, it's more easily testable. So in a world of evidence-based medicine, it's easiest to say that this works. It's cheap. It's quick and so on. Of course, a good clinician and also someone who's well-versed in true science, as opposed to a faith-based, evidence-based medicine, would realize it's much more complex than that.

There are lots of different dimensions. There's all that we know. There's all that we don't know. Most of science is stuff that we don't know we don't know. The common thing is someone will say, "You can't do that because it's not in the guidelines," or "You can't do that because there's not a randomized control trial for it. We can only do what is evidence-based." How do you deal with that? How do you say, "actually life is more complex than that. We operate on many different dimensions, including the wisdom level?"

Jim: I think that's a good question. One looks at the modern medical complex and essentially, it's been taken over by a criminal syndicate of big pharmaceutical companies and reductionist science. More and more, I think medical science is deleterious to human health, rather than therapeutic in any meaningful sense of that term. Here in the United States for example, we are victimized by the criminal syndicate that controls the American Medical Association, controls most of the hospitals. Bruce Lipton, who was a senior professor at Stanford Medical School, he finally resigned because he realized that the medical schools, here in the United States, but I presume it's essentially the same in Great Britain and Europe, are controlled by the big pharmaceutical industries. They're much more interested in selling products that maintain chronic conditions than actually curing people. That's one reason why they have such a rigid, almost militaristic insistence on viewing the body as a machine.

I think a wise doctor coming into such an onerous bureaucratic complexity would have to ask some very fundamental questions about whether he or she belonged there. That's one level because I think all the alternative medicines are much wiser courses and most of the people I know are using the alternative medicine first and if that doesn't work there are, obviously, clear cases where allopathic medicine works, but I think they're less and less effective. At another level, what I would point out to any-body caught up in the scientific paradigm for whom there is no other box, is that if you look at the latest research coming out of science in terms of quantum mechanics, in terms of cosmology etc., what they're discovering is that everything is interconnected with everything else.

For example, Lynne McTaggart who you no doubt know, as a science journalist, has popularized the notion of intention, the power of prayer. Where two or three are gathered together and really focus on sending healing energy to another person, they can measure how that affects the health of the individual who is the focus of that prayer. So I think even reductionist science is coming over and over against that which they most excluded in building reductionist science and that's the reali-ty of consciousness, and how the invisible realms, and the visible realms are interconnected and matter and consciousness are two sides of the same coin. One's intention, one's kindness, one's prayer, one's love for one's neighbor has probably in the end a more contributive effect on healing and health than anything you're going to get through a pill. They've done studies as you may know, where they compared Prozac to placebos, and the placebos are showing themselves more effective in study after study.

Nicholas: I'm assuming that you are not completely saying science is all rubbish, but it's something which is good, but we've over applied it and therefore, it's overshot and gone into areas where …

Jim: I'm saying that science by its very nature is incomplete because it's basic predicate is wrong. It's like when people believed that the earth was flat that worked for most people. It took several hundred years for peo-ple to get that the earth was actually round. When one is using an incomplete predicate that doesn't mean they're completely wrong. It just means that it's incomplete. For science, what science needs to do is un-dergo its own Copernican revolution, in which it understands that the roundness of science is going to be completed when consciousness, when intention, when spirit, when the invisible and the visible are brought to-gether and a third whole emerges that includes and completes both.

That's when science will relax a little and the tyranny of scientific reductionism which is a dogmatic belief, just like evangelical Christianity or radical fundamentalist Islam, it's another dogmatic belief, and like all dogmatic beliefs because it insists on certainties. In a world that is inherently open-ended and mysterious. It has a long way to go. It will get there.

Nicholas: In that process, how does the integration work? Do you see wisdom fitting, interconnecting with logical, empirical rationality in terms of changing the paradigm or changing the hypotheses on which science has done? Or is it two completely different ways of thinking …

Jim: No, again, coming back to my principal definition of wisdom. Wisdom sees the larger context. For example, let's takes someone like Rupert Sheldrake, a good Englishman and a brilliant biologist who's developed the notion of morphogenetic fields, which has been castigated by the prevailing scientific reductionist world, but which in a couple hundred years, say maybe sooner, will be considered normative. When Einstein's physics superseded Newton, there was a lurch in the system and there's more and more scientists like Rupert Sheldrake who are wise, who are deeply scientific, who understand the scientific model. Francis Bacon gave us this notion of the setting forth a hypothesis, doing the tests, drawing tentative conclusions.

Science just needs to understand what Bacon said that it's ultimately theoretical and they made the mistake of thinking that they should limit themselves to only that which is measurable in the five senses. We're learning more and more that we have much more expanded ways of knowing the world and sooner or later, science will go through that Copernican revolution. I believe that the next great frontier of science will in fact be the exploration of consciousness. When that happens, science will come alive for the first time.

Nicholas: In my view, one of the legitimate things science says to defend itself or rather those who have the extremist faith-based reductionist mindset, they'll say science came about and we got rid of medieval superstition or the hocus-pocus potions and bizarre magical belief systems, many of which were nonsense or just either not true, wishful thinking or even abused by powerful people to make money or to seek control. If we're going to say that actually we want to take wisdom back and validate it as something that we hold true in our lives and in our institutions the way we run our world, how do you within wisdom judge what's true and what's false?

If you take the break of scientific rationality off, how do you decide what's true? What's false? What's reasonable? What's not? What's valid?

Jim: I think that's highly personal and I would just note that many of the so-called superstitions and folk cures that were banished in the face of the scientific revolution have turned out to be true. I can still remember when President Nixon went to China and all of a sudden, the United States and the American Medical Association was confronted by the reality of acupuncture. Up to that point, the scientific establishment worldwide said that this was superstitious and it is absolutely untrue.

I can still remember on national television when they showed incontrovertibly that when you put a needle into the body in the calf and the elbow, you can have a patient go through an operation without anesthesia. What we're discovering I think is that science basically got it wrong. Again, rather than trying to stamp out superstition and everything that is not fundamentally scientific so-called, I think that the future of medicine is going to be integral. What we're discovering is that acupuncture in fact, cures a lot, so does homeopathy, so does hypnotism.

Nicholas: The question is actually where does wisdom come in because an empiricist would say ...

Jim: Wisdom is that whole, wisdom is one that holds the whole and the wisdom then from the context, for example of integral medicine then would discern that there's some things that are going to be better treated by big Pharma. There's some things that are going to be better treated by another discipline and again, the wise person holds the whole and synthesizes the different factors that science isn't wrong, the empirical method isn't wrong, it's just one fractal. It's one way of knowing. For example, you come into a room. You instinctively feel an attraction to somebody across the room that you've never met. That's not measurable, but you know something. You go and you see a sunset and you feel the numinosity of the cosmic mystery of light and color and the solar revolutions of the earth around the sun and the sun around the galaxy and you have this epiphanal awareness. You can't measure that, but that's deep mysticism.

As we move into the Twenty-first century, my God, we have to come to an awareness that east and west, north and south, ancient and modern, there have been multiple ways of knowing and wisdom starts with that multiplicity. Then within that context, on a case-by-case basis makes discernments that are requisite and a true for that particular occasion or that particular illness. I think in 50 years we're going to have integral medicine all over the world and a great conversation because in the United States, nearly 50% of the entire population now uses alternative medicine. In case after case, scientific studies Nicholas, Prozac is being beaten by placebos. The deleterious destructive effect of big Pharma on human health, mostly and most egregiously here in the United States where they're even vaccinating babies on their first day of life is becoming more and more apparent, even given the extraordinary measures that the American Medical Association has taken to squelch the information. We have a reformation on our hands and I'm delighted to be able to participate in that through Wisdom University because I think wisdom is much bigger than reductionist science.

Nicholas: Of course, finally if we suppose everyone enrolls in Wisdom University and the wisdom was fully integrated globally, say in 10, 20 years time, what would it be like to live in that world?

Jim: Oh boy, if anybody's interested come to www.wisdomuniversity.org. We have a variety of courses that we hold all over the world, both virtually and in person. I would say that if the world became wise if one could do what no avatar has ever been able to do and click one's finger and people became wise, I would say that in the first instance, we would take seriously that the climate is moving out of control and that we need it as a human race in the next 10 years by 2020 to shift from a fossil-based economy to a renewable energy economy. I would think that all of us individually and as families and communities would begin to focus on sustainability. I think we would start to look at former enemies and understand that we inhabit one single planet and there is plenty of latitude for differences within the context of deep dialogue.

I think a wise world, a wise England, a wise America, a wise France would shift two things. One, the energy that we use to empower our economies and our political infrastructures. Number two, we would realign ourselves with the earth upon which we inhabit. One of the most egregious destructions of fundamentalist science is it's treated the earth on which we live, as dirt that we can literally do anything with. We need to understand Nicholas what James Lovelock says in Gaia, "Gaia, the earth is a living organism." We are her creatures and we have built a scientific modern superstructure on the planet that's predicated on a completely predatory, exploitative, destructive relationship with earth and with other communities. We are marching quickly to our doom.

On the Arctic sea as we speak, there are now plumes of methane erupting out of the sea bed that's been melting because of the receding polar ice caps. Plumes a thousand meters wide which is 30 times more contributive to global warming than even CO_2 are now spewing into the atmosphere and producing millions of tons of methane now into the atmosphere. We're losing control of planet Earth and human civilization is going to be held to account which is going to be terrifying as the turbulence continues to escalate.

So when we talk about the scientific model, when we talk about empirical science, this is no longer a theoretical equation set like $E=MC2$. We're talking about a way of life, a mentality that has been so highly destructive that the Copernican revolution of which I speak cannot come quickly enough. Wisdom is not an ancillary marginal aspect of human affairs. It's become, in my view, a matter of human survival.

Nicholas: These are huge, massive things for an individual person who might be reading, what can they do? What practices or what things can they do in their life to tap into their own wisdom and to contribute to the change that you are talking about?

Jim: I think all of us have an obligation during our tenure on this planet to be as well-informed as we possibly can. I would urge everyone to become informed. Watch the news. Look at what's happening to the weather. Understand the complexity of your world and really spend time connecting the dots. Understand the larger context. I think all of us have a personal and familial and communal obligation to become more sustainable. Go on the website, understand your carbon footprint. Make a commitment to reduce your carbon footprint by 10% this year. Look at how you're living. Look at how you are sustaining your life. Are you engaging in right livelihood? Are you working for a big oil company or a predatory bank? How are you putting food on your table? What's your diet look like?

There are very simple things that individuals and family can do to be much more sustainable, much more humane. When was the last time you went out to nature? When was the last time you contemplated the aliveness of nature or do you just live in a big urban, industrial city like London or New York or Manchester or Glasgow and nature's become something that you see occasionally on television? I think the greatest teacher of wisdom is nature and in fact, it was Whitehead that said that, "Wisdom and nature are never in contradiction with one another." So if there's one thing that I would say to anyone looking at this program is spend as much time in nature feeling the aliveness of Gaia and she will teach you, she will lead you to wisdom.

Nicholas: Thank you very much Jim.

Jim: Thank you so much.

The Living Universe

Bringing Science, Finance and Society to Life

Dr Elisabet Sahtouris interviewed by Dr Nicholas Beecroft
Elisabet Sahtouris is an internationally known Evolution Biologist. In this interview Elisabet inspires us to understand the universe as a conscious, living system. She illustrates this with examples of how the theory applies to finance, falling Western birth rates, welfare systems and medicine. She believes that we're undergoing a new Copernican revolution in science and that that represents a massive opportunity to rebalance the way we live.

With her strong foundation in Western Science, she describes how our science is based upon civilizational assumptions which are in themselves untested but rather based upon faith. She believes that the nonliving universe based upon solely energy and matter is the basic assumption we make without knowing it and she believes that we'd be better of trying out some science based upon the assumption that we are conscious beings living interconnected in a living, conscious universe. She shows how other cultures, especially Indian (Vedic) and Islamic have other assumptions.

She takes us down to the level of bacterial, cells, mitochondria and adenosine-triphosphate to describe the origins of life and the fundamentals of a living system which she then expands up to the level of human society and the universe.

Internationally known as a dynamic speaker, Dr. Sahtouris is an evolution biologist, futurist, professor, author and consultant on Living Systems Design. She shows the relevance of biological systems to organizational design in business, government and globalization. She is a Fellow of the World Business Academy, an advisor to EthicalMarkets.com and the Masters in Business program at Schumacher College, also affiliated with the Bainbridge Graduate Institute's MBA program for sustainable business.

Dr. Sahtouris has convened two International Symposia on the Foundations of Science and written about integral cosmologies. Her books include A Walk Through Time: from Stardust to Us, Biology Revisioned, co-authored with Willis Harman, and EarthDance: Living Systems in Evolution.

Nicholas: Welcome Elisabet to the series Exploring the Future of Western Civilization.

Elisabet: Thank you Nicholas. Nice to be here, talking to you from Spain.

Nicholas: By way of introduction for anyone that doesn't know Elisabet. She's a world famous biologist who has gone on to become a futurist. A pioneer and advocate for a new way of seeing the world as a living system. Is that right Elisabet? Is there anything you would add to that?

Elisabet: No, I think that's just fine. Being an evolution biologist makes you a deep pastist and I think you have to be a deep pastist to be a good futurist. If you know where you've come from, you can have a better of chance of seeing your most reasonably headed.

Nicholas: I heard that you said that you see the multiple crises that we have as a Civilization as an opportunity, as a chance for us to shift to something different and better. Could you say a bit about that? What do you see is possible?

Elisabet: I do see it that way because first of all there have been many crises in our four billion years of earth evolution. Often, really incredible inventive new things came out of those crises. I'd say the reason for that is that crises tend to undo rigidities. Maybe a lot of people listening to this series would know about Arnold Toynbee for instance, the very famous historian who talked about why Civilizations collapse. The two things he spoke of as essential factors where the extreme concentration of wealth which is something we're certainly seeing now ourselves in our current Civilization. Secondly, the refusal to change when change is called for. Clinging to rigid ways of doing things and being unwilling to make changes. It's that brittleness, that rigidity that causes collapses often and then things are opened up. Things become chaotic and chaos gives you the opportunities to reinvent things.

This is one example for instance, we're expecting the major currencies of the world to collapse due to the extremes of wealth concentration by banks. When that happens, when the currencies collapse and your ATM machines don't work one morning, what happens? The field is wide open for reinventing money and for creating ecologies of currencies where you use different currencies for different levels instead of thinking there's only one kind and so on. That would be an example. Examples in nature are the great extinctions. Usually climate changes would knock out up to 95% of living things on the planet. When you look into the fossil record you see complete new ecosystems popping up afterwards because the field was clear again. The niches were unoccupied and new things could happen.

Nicholas: If you look at it in non-individual terms, that makes sense. As individuals, obviously we have our own lives, our own egos and we don't particularly want to be killed or suffer pain or massive upheaval. Is there a way for us to transition to more of a living system way of being without pain and suffering? Is it possible?

Elisabet: I think so. Nicholas, I grew up in the post 1929 depression era and I grew up in a farm country where we were eating completely organic food, although that name didn't exist for it, it was the only kind there was. The chemicals industry hadn't going enough to reach the farms yet. It was just coming in with DDT, the first one. The fact is that we lived very well because we bartered a lot. We didn't depend on money. Different farms had different specialties and they were all within reach of each other so that one would have chicken and eggs and another one had cows and dairy products and another one had fruits and cider mills and honey and things like that. My mother grew a lot of veggies. So it went. Almost everything we needed was grown in abundance on farms. The water tables were never lowered and the soil was always enriched because there were no chemicals. The very fact of growing food always enriched these farms and made them more valuable. There was no expense for the farmer other than his own labor and a certain amount of animal feed. That was easy to balance against the income from selling products.

I would say we're probably going to be forced back to that. I just read a statistic that in the United States, the number of farms had increased for the first time in 150 years. Most of the increase seems to be due to single mothers going back to the land to feed their children. That going back to the land to grow food is now being coupled with lots of community organization all around the world. Communities are getting together and talking about can they get together and buy a windmill, or what kind of energy can they put in as a safety net against the failure of the grid. How many cars are there and what uses are they put to and how they can be shared? What do you do with the school bus at night? Can you use it to take people to restaurants or whatever?

Lots of people now talking about how to sustain themselves at the local level. One of the things that's been long obvious to me as a biologist who always sees humanity as a natural species setting up its own systems of living on the planet, is that you cannot have a healthy global economy at the expense of local economies any more than you could run your body at the expense of your cells. Every cell is fully employed in your body and has to be kept healthy. If any set of cells suffers in the body, the central clearing house of information we call our brains immediately make sure that aid is sent to that part of the body because there's an inherent knowledge in the body that if the entire system isn't well, all of it is in danger. That's something that we really need to learn about our economy is to treat them like living systems rather than mechanized arrangements for making maximum profits from things we produce out of nature. If we don't consume then we toss them. This linear mode of exploiting, producing, consuming and dumping has been deadly.

If we had paid attention to nature, to living systems you would see that economies are always circular that everything is recycled, that what's waste to one species is food to another. That's another way in which we're being pushed now into closing these loops again so that we pay more attention to what we're doing first of all and then we close the loops so that we don't get ourselves into this problem of having exploited the planet to the degree that we're now using more than the planet's ability to replace.

Nicholas: Thinking about the financial system, I had a vision of money as a token of human energy and banks as being repositories of that and that human energy flowing into investments which are human potential;

human energy flowing into human potential. At the moment we measure value in a narrow way according to financial return on investment and benefits for limited stakeholders. I was trying to imagine what it would be like to have a financial system which took a full spectrum living system view of value. I know that you've consulted around the world on that. I wonder if you could say a bit about what a living system bank would be like.

Elisabet: The obvious thing that comes to mind of course is my own body which has 50 to 100 trillion cells and each one of those cells is complex as a large human city which is much easier for us to understand nowadays because most people have been introduced to the concept of fractals where when you go into a complex pattern, any point expands to a full universe. We've all seen movies like Contact where you fly through the universe and you see this tiny dot and it turns out to be a galaxy as you come closer. Within the galaxy, another dot turns out to be an entire star systems surrounded by planets and stuff.

We have this concept now and we can dive in to our cells and see that a single cell is as complex as say a large human city because it contains up to 30,000 of these recycling centers that are closing the economic loop within the culture of the cell, the economy of the cell. About a thousand banks on the average which are called mitochondria. The mitochondria actually have their own DNA and they're the descendants of remote archaea, ancient bacteria that had invented the technology of breathing to make a living. In other words using oxygen. These mitochondrial banks have actual printing presses that print out a currency called ATP, adenosine triphosphate. This currency is common to your entire body and the banks basically are giving out free stored value debit cards. You go to the bank, you check in, they give you the card with a line of debit-ability on it. You go out and spend it into the economy. When you spent it, you're never asked to pay it back. You simply take your empty card back to the bank and they give you a new line. The job of the bank is not just to issue the currency but to carefully regulate the amount in circulation. That's the other part that you need for a healthy currency.

You want to prevent inflation from having too much of the currency around or deflation from not having enough of the currency around. You get the idea. The regulation of the currency is far more important than what backs it.

There's a wonderful movie that you have to hunt around to get the free version online anymore, it's called the Secret of Oz and it's the best film I know on banking that describes why it is important not so much what backs a currency so much as on how to regulate it. Because any barter currency can be issued among people. When I lived in Santa Barbara, California we did Santa Barbara hours modeled on Ithaca hours. We just issue these certificates and they are perfectly legal in the United States as long as you don't call them dollars or make them look like dollars. You simply give away this currency and get people to start trading it with each other. Currency is an agreement among people that any token has value, getting back to your issue of value.

We pegged it to the dollar in the sense of saying an hour of work was worth $10 at that time. You don't have to do that, you don't have to peg it. The main problem with the banking system today is that very, very little of the money being exchanged around the world in this giant global casino that it's become has anything to do with real economy. What is the value of money when it turns out that the worst mortgages, the ones that were least likely to be paid back by the people who bought them are the most lucrative instruments to trade among the bankers and investors? It has become an absolutely bizarre system at this point. It has nothing to do with the real economy, but it can sink the real economy if people take it seriously enough. In other words, when your ATM machine one morning and very possibly sometime during the coming year, doesn't work anymore. The money you're used to has essentially become unavailable or useless. There are just as many people, just as much human energy, just as much land, just as many productive facilities. Nothing in the physical world changes the day that announcement is made. Theoretically, any local community or nation could immediately issue a currency for the nation or for the local community to keep people doing what they were doing. No one would suffer, there would be no recession.

Nicholas: With the system you were just describing, obviously one of the functions of currency is to be a measure of value. In that system you talked about. For example, if there's a plumber who's got skills that people really need and there aren't many and he's in real demand, how would the regulation work to regulate the availability of his services?

Elisabet: Obviously, if he's a scarce resource his value will go up.

Nicholas: If people just go back to the bank and say give me more….

Elisabet: That's what I said. I said the bank will regulate how much you get the next time around. The bank will only issue the currency in the amount needed to keep the economy in balance. It is not intended to expand. Your body is an expanding economy only up until its full size. Once your body is mature, it shifts into a sustainability mode, not a growth mode any longer. That's exactly what we need to do now, to shift our economy from a growth mode profit seeking, first and foremost profit seeking system to one that brings it into balance among humans and with all other species and resources as we call them natural features of the planet like fresh water and clean air and so forth.

I wanted to say Charles Eisenstein's new book, Sacred Economics goes very beautifully into what would a currency of the future look like. His proposal is that you do back the currency but you back it with the things that you want most on the planet when you're behaving like an intelligent living system. What you would do is back the currency with the amount of oil you leave in the ground, with the amount of gold you leave in the ground, with the amount of fresh air that you still have on the planet, the forests. All of those things that we want to increase the value of and that we want people to increase, to make more of, to ensure more of.

There are a gazillion ways that you can set up currencies with no backing, with just as an agreement among people, with rules of transaction or with something like we have today or with something like what Charles is suggesting.

Nicholas: You talked about regulation and if you think about issues of fairness, you mentioned the disparity between the very wealthy and the poor. Also, if you look at the welfare system that that's a very industrial- ized system, isn't it? Treating people as objects and done it at a very transactional and bureaucratic way. To actually get forward to a more honest system that's genuinely fair but also, for example, doesn't allow free loading or free riding and so on. How does nature do that? How does nature balance competition and cooperation to ensure fairness?

Elisabet: First of all, the main value of a natural system like and an eco- system. I don't mean value to us, it's values. It's internal values. Whether it's a rainforest or a human body is health and survival. A healthy sus- tainability is the main value. When you look at healthy sustainability, you see that you can't have rich and poor. You can't have a couple of organs in your body feeding of the rest of the organs to keep themselves healthy because they know that they would be killing themselves. In fact, when that happens, when cells refuse to negotiate with the rest of the system anymore and just keep reproducing themselves, we call it cancer. We know it's an anomaly and that it threatens the entire system. We have a cancerous banking system in the world today.

Nicholas: A few a years ago I was lucky enough to spend some time in Botswana and it was fascinating to see just how the amazing diversity of nature but also how every single thing eats every other single thing and no one was safe.

Elisabet: Yes, in nature things feed off each other but it's in a complete- ly recycling form and it's usually set up in such a way that increases the health of the system. For example, all predator prey relationships are set up so that the predators job is to keep the prey species healthy by eating only the weakest members of it and keeping it in balance, preda- tor and prey relationships. If the predator eats too much then there's not enough food left for him. If it eats too little then the prey species may get unhealthy. It literally has the job of calling the prey species in such a way that it stays healthy.

There's a lovely example of that. I met a beautiful lady named Sarah James who is a Gwich'in Indian from the northernmost village of Alaska in the Arctics, up there in the Arctic Circle. Their culture was a caribou culture. They were entirely dependent on caribou for their sustenance.

They made their houses, their clothing, their snow shoes, their kayaks, their music instruments, their cups there, everything was made from caribou besides eating the meat to sustain themselves as well.

They loved the caribou, the caribou are their brothers. They did everything possible to keep the caribou healthy. They fed them and they culled only the weak ones. I've talked to Siberian hunters who, when they trained, are never ever allowed to take the first animal they see nor they ever allow it to take the biggest animal they see. They're carefully taught to hunt so that nothing in the ecosystem becomes unhealthy.

Nicholas: People have got in trouble in the past with using evolution-ary ideas, haven't they? You could apply what you just said to culling the weak and sick in the human population. Instead of a health service and a welfare system, you could have a culling system.

Elisabet: The first order of business is to keep people healthy. Humans come in with a different set of values or an expanded set of values. If humans really did practice love, certainly they would not be killing each other nor do you see species in nature killing their own kind. It's very rare in nature in any species that it kills its own kind. There are cases or male cats killing off baby kittens, but maybe in the larger scheme of things, they are forced into that when there's over breeding. I don't know. I don't want to get into that. We tend to think it's nasty in nature that things eat each other. I challenge anybody to think up a better living system than one that endlessly recycles its own molecules. I don't know how you could have a living system without having a serious recycling system. Recycling includes making a living for each other.

I've worked with many indigenous cultures who never took an animal from nature without a polite request for volunteers in that animal spe-cies. They were able to commune with the other species. The hunters would dream the hunt and anthropologists would go and see the hunter sleeping under a tree for a couple of days and say, "Man, are the-se lazy people? Aren't they ever going to get up and hunt?" Meanwhile the hunter had taught the young man tracking and bows and arrows and all those things. He would come out of the dream and say it's a young female elk who is sterile for some reason and she has a notch in her right front hoof and she's three bends down the river on the left bank waiting.

Nicholas: Actually, Elisabet, it's funny that you mentioned communing with animals because by the way of preparation for this interview talking about the world as a living system, I went to fields nearby where I knew that I would be able to spend some time with some horses and the beautiful trees around. Things didn't go quite as planned because I came across a new Gypsy encampment which I hadn't seen before near where I lived. It made me wonder, that situation is one which is very contentious in our society. When people see Gypsies turn up on the edge of their village or town, there are different lenses through which they look and that can be quite controversial. They may look through a security lens and think about potential crime. They could look at it through a fairness lens as to who has the right to live on what land or ownership. Who owns what land, planning permission, that kind of thing. You could look at it through the liberal diversity lens of different types of people living in harmony, getting to know one another. Different cultures living in parallel. You could look at it through a Marxist lens, different power structures and so on.

Could I put that scenario to you Elisabet and say when a group of Gypsies turn up on the edge of a town, what is the living system perspective that describes the relationships that they have with the rest of the community?

Elisabet: First of all, you can't immediately make a living system out of a nonliving system. Yes, we are a living system simply because we too are humans, we too are part of nature. We have so denied that that we have set up a situation in which the Gypsies come in as invasive humans that don't belong in that part of the system. If we were truly operating like a coherent living system then there would be no outsiders and there would be welcomed in for their creativity and negotiation would happen between them and the system they were coming into. We would have to decide, are they guests? Do we ask them to do a certain of work in turn for renting the land? Do we want to negotiate with them to use a different piece of land? There would be friendly negotiation, not hostile approaches and fear of each other and things like that.

Nicholas: Do you think so? Of the people who would agree with what you're saying generally about this moving towards a conscious living system, there are those who would do it from an integral perspective. Many would see it from a pseudo-liberal perspective. With a lot of the baggage of Christianity, a lot of the guilt that comes with that.

Elisabet: You're saying it Nicholas. We have so much baggage on so many levels of things that we simply have gotten very far away from the way natural systems function. I maintain that in the hundred thousand years that we were human, we perfected the tribal level of things quite well so that there were loads of situations around the world where tribes lived peaceably in each other's neighborhoods and there was a negotiation of territory, of boundaries. There were certainly no ideas of ownership of land, ownership of land is a very weird concept. That's another thing by the way that Charles talks about in Sacred Economics, Charles Eisenstein that in the future we can't do that anymore. We can't own property as pieces of land on this planet. You can perhaps own the things that people make out of natural ecosystems, but not the land itself that you're on.

You have to go way back to so many of the things that we have thought up about how to run our economies. I crusade hard for a real science of economics. We do not have one. Our economic theories are all based on the most superficial Darwinism. In my view is an evolution biologist, Darwin only dealt with the youthful expansionist mode economics species and completely ignored the ones that had gone into mature cooperative sustainability. Kropotkin who was widely in the Soviet Union acknowledged Darwin for his work and then looked at the cooperative part of evolution. You can find both competition and cooperation in evolution. To me, you have to put the two together and see a maturation curve. That's exactly what would be so useful for us today to say, "It's not that we're bad for having done capitalism, it's just that we're prolonging our adolescence past where it's sustainable. We have to move now into a cooperative maturity."

Part of the reason why we have been so blind is because science ignored nature's real economies and because science in general has had a very limited view of how nature works. I know that you're interested in paradigms. Do you want to get into that?

Nicholas: Yes, actually. As you know, I'm a psychiatrist and I was in a discussion with some colleagues the other day and someone brought up the subject of using whale music, listening to whales as a therapy. Immediately, there were chortles and titters around the room. There was a general discrediting of the idea without even considering it. It struck me as a very non-evidence based and unscientific response. I'm pretty sure no one there had ever read a scientific study on the therapeutic benefits of whale music and certainly not a randomized control trial.

I did think quietly, I don't know anything much about the clinical or psychological benefits of listening to whale music, but I'd be amazed if it wasn't beneficial, from my own experience. I'm sure there haven't been randomized control trials, but I'm pretty sure at the very least it must be relaxing which has got huge benefits and probably a much deeper spirit level action. I thought, probably, I reckon a third of the people in the room privately have got whale CDs at home. (laughing) They wouldn't tell anyone.

Elisabet: If I could just, just before we go off that topic let me a share a little story. I am in touch again with a dear friend who was Lockheed's chief missile scientist. He was the one who developed the interceptor missile and got lots of awards in Washington during the Reagan years. He had a whale dream many years ago and has been communion; I distinguish between deep communion of direct mind to mind transmission and communication which requires our formal languages and writing and what we're doing here in the internet and all that.

He's in touch with whales all the time that he's in the non-time space realm where distance doesn't make a difference. There you go, a top missile scientist, engineer. His life, his deep soul life is nurtured completely by this communion with whales.

Ok, now, paradigms. How do we see the world? How do we see nature? You're interested in the paradigm shift to living systems obviously, that's what you've been asking me about.

First of all, we have to be very clear, what do we mean by a paradigm. Secondly, what is a shift in a paradigm? Of course, the idea comes from

Thomas Kuhn's 1962 book, The Structure of Scientific Revolutions showing that science has been moving in a progression from understanding the world in what we now think of as primitive ways to more sophisticated ways. We went from the earth-centered universe to the solar-centered universe to the Omni-centric universe. Of course, Giordano Bruno was burned at the stake for proposing an Omni-centric universe long before these shifts took place.

Anyway, we know that that happens. What is the paradigm itself that is shifting when in this paradigm shift is a set of assumptions about the universe you are studying. You can't build a science on nothing. You cannot make a theory in science about a universe you have no conception of. You wouldn't know how to formulate a theory about it, would you? Science has to choose certain things to say about a universe, certain basics about a universe. What these are the things that at any given cultural time, when founding fathers of science are thinking these things up, are to them obvious. I know this because when I give a talk about living universe, a scientist may saunter up to me and say, "I loved your poetic metaphors." If you use organic metaphors, they're poetic. If you use mechanical metaphors, they are real, right? He said, "This of course isn't really science you're talking about. Is it?" I say, "Why do you say that?" They say, "Because you can't prove it." I say, "Prove what?" They say, "You can't prove this is a living universe." I say, "How did you prove this was nonliving universe?" While they're taken it back for a moment, they snap back very quickly saying, "We don't have to." I say, "Why?" They say, "It's obvious." The paradigm is the obvious at that particular cultural time space level, whatever you want to call it, historical point.

What are these fundamental axioms of Western science? They are things like, "This is a nonliving universe." The universe is made of matter and energy. It is measurable. It can be studied objectively. Consciousness is a late emergent product of its interactions and so on. That constitutes a basic world view and are the unproven foundational assumptions that underpin the science.

I have a mission in this life. First of all, to get Western science to acknowledge that these are unproven assumptions and to make them public, the unproven assumptions so that they can distinguish between those and the theories and the tests and all the experimental research. I believe that sciences are distinguished by these sets of assumptions and not by the methodologies. Scientific methodology is scientific methodology and there's a wide variety of it but you can decide whether something is legitimately scientific in its methodology or not.

I wanted to trace this paradigm shift and I held a symposium in Japan because a wonderful Japanese scientist and businessman sponsored it there. We brought them people from around the world who are scientists and philosophers of science all of which I knew to have made a paradigm shift already to a different set of assumptions that this was a conscious universe, that matter arose from consciousness rather than the other way around, consciousness arising from matter; that it was not possible to be completely objective as a scientist because it's a participatory universe and so on. I had them list, very clearly write out, all the fundamental assumptions they were taught and all the fundamental assumptions that they had shifted to look at the paradigm shift.

In the middle of that symposium, I had an epiphany. I said, "Wait a minute." What I am doing is talking about how in evolutions species mature from fierce competition to healthy collaboration, to sustainable cooperation. I'm talking a conquest if I'm talking replacement. Maybe, our world view should be an alternative, the basis for an alternative science rather than a replacement science. That would be cooperation rather than conquest. I very quickly came on the idea of what we need just as the religions have world parliaments of religions, we need a consortium of global sciences. The next symposium I held was in Kuala Lumpur for Islamic scientists and philosophers of science and I had them write out their fundamental assumptions and they're so quite different again. It starts with number one, Allah created the universe, and number two is Allah created a living universe. Bingo, we have a living universe to study now.

We have already three sciences. The one that we call the paradigm shift, the Western, we, I count myself as one of those scientist trained in Western science but having adopted essentially the unproven assumptions of Vedic science from India. This is not a surprise because many scientist and including people like Fritjof Capra and Rupert Sheldrake trained in Western science went to India. Also, of course poets and hip-pies and everybody else went and they brought back gurus and brought back yoga. A very long standing scientific practice, meditation. All of these things came into our culture along with these different fundamental assumptions.

My mission is, let's see how to create a consortium of sciences. I thought, "How can I get Western scientist to understand this whole thing about the assumptions and that sciences would be distinguished by them and that they stand on their own set of them that aren't often acknowledged." I decided I needed to do the research in order to be convincing. I've got Globescan in London lined up. They're a very effective global polling organization, research organization doing mostly market research. They're very interested in developing an instrument and doing the research around the world to demonstrate that people with Ph.Ds in Western science who are out there teaching and practicing actually hold rather different assumptions about the universe, depending specially on their culture.

Who's to say, which human view of the universe is right and which is wrong. I think it's dangerous to have the hegemony of one science that has this limited materialistic world view because, for example, when it starts to mess with life, it doesn't understand life well. It understands machinery beautifully but it doesn't understand life. It doesn't understand the differ-ence between a mechanical heart pump and the heart that is in your body, alive and can't be put on a table and kept going forever.

When they mess around with genetic engineering, with high-tech agri-culture, with a lot of pharmaceuticals and stuff like that, they need a parallel equal science based on living systems to be able to say, "Look, you're out of bounds here." Your foundations don't permit you to do the kind of theorizing and concluding that we do. You could see what's unhealthy.

Nicholas: One of the things that made me decide to embark on this project exploring the Western mind, the evolution of the Western mind was that I noticed that we actually massively lack diversity, genuine true diversity, not politically correct diversity. You would have thought that across the whole Western world, of course the whole world, there ought to be lots and lots of people experimenting with different types of schools, different types of leadership, different types of healthcare. Actually, when you look around there's an amazing groupthink. For example, psychiatry, the way it's done is incredibly limited.

Elisabet: In the dominant culture, but of course, around the dominant culture there still are pockets of amazing diversity in all of these things. I was in Dharamsala with the Dalai Lama one time and went to the Museum of Tibetan Medicine up there. It was mind-boggling to see the medical texts. They were as rich and as richly illustrated and microscopically detailed as anything in Western science. A whole museum of these big textbooks on Tibetan science which of course was Ayurvedic science and was connected with India and all other cultures. The Buddhists and the Hindus got together on a lot of these things overtime.

Nicholas: As you're talking, I was thinking of two dimensions where I've often been in conflict with others. One has been around what's called evidence based medicine. The notion that medicine should be based upon good science and should have proven techniques and so on. Obviously, as an idea you couldn't possibly disagree with that. The trouble is when you dig down into it, the quality of the science, the narrowness of the areas which have been studies to the narrowness of the questions. The lack of strength of the statistics...

Elisabet: ... and the profit motive.

Nicholas: ... and the profit motive. Fundamentally, what you were saying about the underlying assumptions. Once you actually factor all of that in, you're dealing with castles built in the sky.

The trouble is, particularly the way it's done in psychiatry, people keep talking about evidence based medicine which basically means giving people pills and cognitive behavior therapy. It frustrates me because it's so unbelievably limited. If you challenge it, they just say, "Well that's science."

My question is would you spends time trying to persuade, trying to resist or would you just leave and going to do your own thing?

Elisabet: Well I left long ago. (laughter) I taught for a little while at MIT in the University of Massachusetts and I've done a postdoctoral at the Museum of Natural History in New York. By the way, that was when Roger Payne first brought in whales song recordings. Then I practiced for a while at Mass. General Hospital doing research and then in some of the Boston think tanks, people who answered research proposals from the government and stuff. I just left, I went to Greece. I decided I would read novels to explain the human condition to myself because science wasn't answering my big questions about who we humans were, where we came from, and where we're headed, which I thought was so important. The museum was belching black smoke over all of North Manhattan. While down in the great hall of the American Museum of Natural History was a very expensively built Japanese designed pollution exhibit.

The contradictions became obvious and I made myself unpopular by pointing them out. I decided to go and write novels, as I said, to explain the human condition to myself. While walking in the forest and a little island I was living on that was still beautifully forested largely because it had been a leper colony in the past. The developers avoided it. I knew I still wanted to be a scientist. I needed to put story of evolution together for myself. That ended up as my book, Earthdance Living Systems and Evolution.

Seeing nature as intelligent and seeing evolution as an improvisational dance. Seeing that the first half of evolution, two billion years, were devoted to the archaea, the ancient bacteria that proved to be more like us humans than anything in between. One of my pet projects, it's on the agenda now, is I want to do a film for kids called "Bacteria Are Us" on the back of "Toys R Us." They, our cells, are the cooperatives that they built when they got over their hostilities. These ancient bacterias were the only ancient beings on this planet until we came along to cause global hunger, global pollution, climate change, and they solved these problems. They harnessed solar energy to make food and maintain photosynthesis. They invented breathing to make a living by smashing food molecules the way we do. That's why these mitochondrial descendants are still in our cells. We have at least ten times as many bacteria in our guts and on our skins and as are trapped in our cells as mitochondria, descendants of ancient free-living bacteria. It's turning out that our gut bacteria regulate up to eighty percent of our immune systems.

If that gets out among the public, I would think, parents would think twice before they take their kids to the fast food shop again. Anyway, I believe we're going to be pushed back into more local food sustainability and stuff. The diet will improve, the health will improve. It is not the worst thing in the world to face the kind of crisis that we're facing that will drive us back to basics. I want to take along our computers. I say to young people, we can't all be organic farmers. We want the techies. We just have to figure out how to make computers completely recyclable and not to put any toxins in them in the first place. I believe we have all the creativity and ingenuity to do that. There are as many ways to build a better world as there are creative individuals to work on it. I advise people to love what they're doing to make a better world in such a way that their work is attractive to others. Others will say, "Oh, they're having fun. What are they doing?" and want to join them.

We can't force it on each other. We have to, I happen to like the word seduce, seduce each other into making a better world, into understanding the benefits of living like a really healthy mature living system on the planet. To build a real global family where we don't waste any energy on making war anymore and weapons and all that stupidity that's a complete waste of human energy.

I think it's all possible. I'm excited about the crises. I even celebrate them. Being compassionate about those suffering. Knowing that if we took my attitude, we would be more proactive. Right now, the best informants I have say there's not a single corporation the world that has a clue have to stop any of these crises. There's not a single government that's prepared for the emergencies they will cause people. We really need to wake up and acknowledge that we're in crisis. Acknowledge that we've overstepped our limits on the planet and that we can still create paradise on earth in terms of living cleanly and adequately, all of us. No one left out. Global family. There is enough for all. Enough as Gandhi said, "For our need if not for our greed."

Nicholas: Looking at the human system through the biological lens, I was interested to know what you think about relative birth rates. Generally speaking, human birth rates were very high and have been coming down rapidly, particularly so in the West. The birth rates in Islamic and

African countries remain relatively high. Some people would just say that's just because, in terms of cultural evolution, they're behind the curve. They'll catch up. They are catching up.

Elisabet: If you permit them to catch up, they'll catch up. We're preventing the kind of catch up that we should be allowing. I know where you're headed Nicholas and we have so little time. I'm going to jump in and say, never look at population without looking at consumption. The average American in the United States consumes about forty times what a Bangladeshi does.

Nicholas: No, my question is, is the fact that those cultures have got a higher birth rate, is that a sign that they're way of life and their beliefs is more in tune with life? Maybe we're dying off because we're not.

Elisabet: As humans, I would say it's because they're insecure and uneducated. It's been demonstrated that one year of education for a girl in a place like Africa or Bangladesh is one less baby. It's not just because they're sitting in school. It's because they will just have a whole different outlook on life and what the value of them is. It's a matter of getting the value that they are contributors to their economies, not just baby makers. The insecurity is, you have twelve children hoping one will survive to take care you in old age when you can't work. The culture doesn't take care of you. We all know that what brings the birth rate down most effectively is development. Why aren't we developing the people we're upset about breeding too much? Why aren't we encouraging and facilitating their development? Instead of only giving what we call aid which always has huge strings attached.

I've read Confessions of an Economic Hitman. Colonialism was primitive compared to the way we do it today. We've got to end this culture of greed and go into the value of every human being treating them well. The population rate will go down mostly because of the disasters now. I would prefer it to go down through healthy development.

Nicholas: That's not quite I meant. What I meant was, if you look at the, as we call ourselves, advanced Western scientists, also Russia, also Japan and China, we are well below the population replacement rate.

Elisabet: Nicholas, so did primitive tribes, as we call them primitive. They knew how to balance their population within their ecosystems and they did it.

Nicholas: The question is, do you interpret the drop in the birth rates at the biological level as a sign, as feedback saying, "The planet's full and we're running out of resources and therefore....

Elisabet: ....Yes. Africa wasn't overpopulating before colonialism. We inflicted that insecurity on them. We took the men and boys out of the villages and put them in factories and mines and mega farms and stuff. Exploited everybody, broke up their communities, destroy their values, and made it impossible for them to remain in their ecosystems in balance.

Nicholas: That's still not the point though.

Elisabet: It's still not?

Nicholas: No. I'm not making value judgments about African's or Muslims or colonialism. I'm just saying, in terms of the healthiness of our ecosystem, our way of being. Looking at with the Western societies and Russia, and Japan and actually increasingly China. We dropped our birth rates below replacement levels so that place like Italy and Russia are halving in terms of their domestic population each generation.

Looked at through a biological lens, is that a sign of nature saying, "Look, there are too many of you. You need to cut down." That's one hypothesis. Or, is it a sign that our way of life has lost contact with life and so we're not bothering to reproduce? The fact that the others have higher birth rates is a sign that their cultures are more in touch with life.

Elisabet: We need to restore ourselves as healthy living systems and then population will automatically adjust. When we behave like a healthy living system, your cells don't overproduce, elephants don't overreproduce. Living systems in balance are in balance and we're out of balance. We need to rebalance ourselves and those problems will take care of themselves. They will evaporate.

Nicholas: Thank you very much. It's been a real pleasure to talk to you. I really enjoyed that. Just finally, if someone wants to follow up your work or make contact with you, how would you recommend they do that?

Elisabet: My website has lots of free stuff including the Earthdance Living Systems in Evolution, a whole copy of that and many articles and videos and stuff. It is simply my last name www.sahtouris.com. There's an e-mail button there. I wish everyone a wonderfully healthy balanced life.

Nicholas: Great. Thank you.

Organizational Democracy

10 Steps to Democratic Culture and Leadership

Traci Fenton interviewed by Dr Nicholas Beecroft

Traci Fenton is an expert in organizational democracy and the Founder and CEO of WorldBlu whose purpose is to unleash human potential and inspire freedom by championing the growth of democratic organizations worldwide. Her vision is to see 1 billion people working in free and democratic workplaces. Traci describes the ten principles which make an organization democratic-from modern entrepreneurial companies to the US Navy and CIA. Democratic culture in the workplace leads to improved engagement, creativity, productivity, meaning, health, energy and profit. She says where it works and where it doesn't; who's ready and who's not. Worldblu supports businesses to transition from a Command and Control Model of organization to an empowering democratic model by showing the structures, processes, rules, values, consciousness and type of leadership that are necessary to support democratic culture? She discusses how democracy can improve profits, strategy, governance, decision making, accountability and risk management.

Nicholas: Traci, welcome to the series, Exploring the Future Western Civilization.

Traci: It's great to be here. Thanks for having me, Nick.

Nicholas: My pleasure. If anyone hasn't heard of Traci or WorldBlu, Traci Fenton is the CEO and founder of WorldBlu. This is a company in the United States that's going global and its purpose is to unleash human potential and inspire freedom by championing the growth of democratic organizations worldwide.

As part of that Traci and her colleagues produced the WorldBlu list which is a list of the most democratic workplaces around the world, those who are the most transparent collaborative and decentralized.

Her bold vision is to have one billion people working in free and demo-cratic workplaces within, I think it's within your lifetime isn't it?

Traci: Yes. I'm going to see it.

Nicholas: Is there anything you'd add to that or is that about it?

Traci: That's probably it although I'll say we do have an office in London too. We have members in 60 countries globally so we really, really are global organizations. Glad to be here with you today.

Nicholas: Obviously, I gave a mini introduction but would you mind saying, basically your elevator pitch, what is WorldBlu and what are you doing?

Traci: Sure. WorldBlu is really a global network of companies that stand for this idea of freedom and democracy in the workplace. This is in contrast to the command and control model of business which is how most companies have been structured.

The command and control model arguably worked for the industrial age but we're not in the industrial age anymore. I think we moved from the industrial age into the information age, right? As we all know, the infor-mation age has given birth to a new age which is the democratic age.

We're in the age of unprecedented transparency and opportunities to collaborate and participate and have influence unlike anything we've seen before. The leaders, these company leaders and people who are saying, "There has to be different way of doing business in this new age that we're in." Guess what? It's democracy. It really should have been democracy all along.

Now we're in an age with these outside trends that are really causing corporate leaders to say, "We need a model that's going to be more efficient, more adaptable, attract and retain top talent and that's organi-zational democracy.

WorldBlu is certifying organization, we're a membership organization and we have a consulting arm as well.

Nicholas: Great. Now I know that when you say democracy you don't mean voting on every single thing. You set out some very clear principles of what democracy is and what it isn't. Could you summarize that?

Traci: Sure, when you hear the word democracy most people think politics and that's what I thought too when I first started to fall in love with this idea. When you actually get in to understanding what democracy is, it's about creating an environment that unleashes human potential because it's built on the principles of freedom rather than fear or control.

We're not talking about politics, we're not even talking about voting. Voting or consensus based decision making are just that. They're ways of making a decision but they're not the entire ecology of what democracy is.

Under Saddam Hussein, they could vote in Iraq for their leader. Does that make that a democracy? Of course not. We need to have a more sophisticated understanding of what democracy, organizational democracy actually is and hopefully we can get into that today.

Nicholas: I know that you have 10 principles that you measure companies against, 10 benchmarks.

Traci: Yes, yes. I started WorldBlu in 1997, 15 years ago. I can't believe how time flies. I really spent those first 10 years of WorldBlu just researching and setting out to understand what democracy is. Many people look at democracy as a set of practices.

Again, back to voting or consensus or separation of powers. What I found in my research is it's not about a uniform cookie-cutter approach to practicing it. It's about understanding the principles that create the system. Here I am in the US, you're in the UK, we both, we share the same language, we both are democratic societies, but the way we practice it looks different but the principles are the same and they're universal principles.

I wanted to know what are those principles? I started with 27 and the research came down, came down, came down and really identified the

10 core principles and they're on our website, WorldBlu.com. They're principles like transparency accountability, choice, decentralization of power, the balance of the individual and the collective, purpose and vision, dialogue and listening, and so on and so forth.

The key point to remember here is that all 10 of those principles have to be practiced to truly have a democratic environment. This isn't, pick your favorite three. That may make it a nice place to work but it's not going to be a sustainable, democratic ecology where you're really going to be able to get the most out of it.

Nicholas: Traci, I know you've done a lot of research on what it is that makes a democratic organizational culture. I wonder if you could lay those out for us.

Traci: Absolutely. Here are the 10 principles of organizational democracy that we've identified. Number one is purpose and vision, number two is transparency, three is dialogue and listening, four is fairness and dignity, five is accountability, six is individual and collective, seven is choice, eight is integrity, nine is decentralization, and ten is reflection and evaluation.

Nicholas: Traci, why is democracy in the workplace important? Why does it matter?

Traci: This is a very important question and it's important from a couple different angles and perspectives. Let's start first with business leaders and managers. CEOs, leaders, owners of businesses, they want to know how do I run a more efficient business. How do I make it more productive, more innovative?

How do I not only attract top talent to my workplace, how do I keep it so you don't have to deal with high turnover rates? And quite frankly, how do I make more money? We all need business. It's how we all live.

Companies are always asking, "How do we get better at this?" This organizational democracy is the framework for how to be better. I don't think there's that many great frameworks out there that have really said how to do it. Again, I think that previous models have been based on the military model, the command and control model.

Number one, it's a more effective model for basing the bottom line. Number two, it's for employees. Employees are going to benefit. I mean I would much rather live in a democratic society than live in a dictatorship and that's how people feel about their workplace too.

We all know what it's like to have that horrible boss. My first job out of college was for a Fortune 500 company and I walked in to work the first day ready to engage and participate, excited about that first job as many of us feel. By the end of day one I left feeling completely dehumanized. I felt like it was just going to be a toxic work environment. They're going to use about one percent of my capabilities, it was awful.

As an employee I don't want to work in that kind of workplace. I want to work in a democratic workplace where I can have a voice, where I can a contribution, where I feel like I can have ideas and give them, send them forth and be recognized for them.

There's a benefit to employees. Then there's also a benefit to the world to be perfectly honest and this isn't just some nice Kumbayah idea. There is research, some wonderful research that Gretchen Spreitzer at the University of Michigan Business School has conducted that can quantify that when an organization operates democratically, it increases the level of peace, economic prosperity and civic engagement in a community. So when a company operates on these principles you're impacting the leaders, you're impacting the employees' lives, you're impacting the global society. I think that's a pretty good case for why is this so important.

Nicholas: What you say about engagement and empowerment, in other words, if you have an environment which really liberates the soul or the spirit, engages the passions of people; I have read over the years lots of research that backs that up that says that means more creativity, more money, more profit, more success, better ideas, less sick leave and all that sort of thing. Why is it that people don't do it?

Traci: I don't know. The research is out there that proves that more

179

engagement, all of these things benefit the bottom line. I mean according to the Gallup Organization, 73 percent of the US workforce is disengaged at work and I know that there are similar numbers across the board. Europe is even higher, same in Japan. This costs the US economy $300 billion a year. You would think, "Well duh, let's engage people."

I think there's usually two reasons why we hit the wall. The first reason is ego. Our egos don't understand. We think we have to hold on to power. We think power is finite rather than understanding it can be shared, it's an infinite thing and that it's like, it sounds kind of cheesy but it's like when you light a candle you light someone else's candle, you still have your candle.

It might sometimes change form but instead of power, this kind of power, it's that open power but it's still power that you can have as a leader because you're empowering others. It's the ego that tries to stop us and make up a whole story around why we can't go on this path. The other thing that of course tries to stop us is just ignorance of how to do it. I hope that's what WorldBlu and the framework can do for people is give them a map, a chart, a way of actually implementing this that takes out the fear and is very empowering to them.

Nicholas: Could you give an example of a couple of places where you've seen democracy in the workplace really working, thriving, to give us a feel for what it's like?

Traci: Well, we have several companies over in the UK that have been certified as WorldBlu democratic companies and let me tell you about one of them. We'll start at your side of the pond and I have plenty of stories to tell.

One of my favorite democratic companies is called NixonMcInnes and they are a social media company that is based in Brighton, UK. I love Brighton. I'd been down to their offices many, many times. They have a wonderful CEO named Will McInnes. He's done quite a bit of talking about these ideas. You can Google him and learn more.

There's quite a few ways that they practice organizational democracy. One of them is this idea of transparency and decentralization. They have something called the money gang. What they do is they have this group of folks that's elected by the company, small group, that gets together and they look at the books that the books are open to the company. Everyone's salaries are open and the money gang gets together. They look at the books and they say, "Is everyone being treated fairly here when it comes to compensation?"

If people want to be paid more or if they want to talk about their salary, they come to the money gang and the money gang reviews it. The money gang approves everyone's salary including the CEO to make sure that there's a sense of fairness and dignity. There's this transparency. Nobody is gaming the system. I think it's a really bold way of practicing organizational democracy. They do another thing that's kind of fun.

Nicholas: Sorry, just to interrupt with you. With that, is the CEO in that group?

Traci: In the actual money gang? No, he's not.

Nicholas: He doesn't have a veto?

Traci: No, that's right, but his salary is reviewed by the money gang, which I love.

Nicholas: The ability to decide how much people get paid is a very powerful lever, isn't it? How has that affected the dynamics of the company?

Traci: Well, I think what it's done, when you walk in there, you walk in NixonMcInnes, they've got these bright, fun colored walls and open space and there's a dynamism, there's an energy, there's a trust. They've got about 20 employees or so and they're quite successful. They work with major, major clients there in the UK.

A couple of their other practices that I think are just really fun and work for them and their size. They have something called these happy buckets. As he walks out the door and I've seen them myself, there's a bucket, a purple bucket that has an 'H' written on a piece of paper sitting on the bottom and a blue bucket that has a 'U' sitting on a piece of paper sitting on the bottom of the bucket and the third bucket which is a bucket of tennis balls.

As you leave work each day, you take your tennis ball and you put it in one of those buckets. Are you either happy or unhappy? They're voting if you will on the temperature of the organization. If there's a majority of balls are so in the happy bucket, why are they happy, let's talk about what's working. If the majority of buckets is unhappy, let's talk about it. What's going on? That I think is really fun.

One other practice I'll share with you around the principle of reflection and evaluation. I just learned about this when I was at their office in November, is something they do called, "The Church of Fail" and what they do is they take one of their conference rooms and they take the chairs, put them together into rows like the pews in a church.

One by one they're invited to get up in front of everyone and confess their sins about something they did that month where they "failed." As they share and have their confessionals the audience hoots and hollers and cheers them on. Of course the idea here is to create an atmosphere that eliminates fears where people can learn together. We're all listening, we're all thinking that let's share how we learned and live on.

Nicholas: Traci, with the Church of Fail, what needs to be in place by way of structure, praise and leadership for that to be safe because then I'd say in the majority of workplaces, certainly those I've been in, if you did that you'd open yourself up to attack and it'd be quite …

Traci: Terrifying isn't it?

Nicholas: … dangerous to be honest like that. What needs to happen to make that possible?

Traci: It's a very good point because your readers can't go and say, I'm going to start a Church of Fail tomorrow in my extremely messed up company and everything is going to be great. No. You need to ease into this. What it really is about is again taking the principles and finding practices for those principles that's appropriate for the stage that you're at.

It's very good to start with purpose and vision, having a very clear sense. Most companies know what their mission is and a mission is what we do but the purpose is what we be. It's the being. Why does an organization exist?

WorldBlu exists to elevate the human spirit. What do we do? We promote democracy in the workplace. We certify companies. What's our vision? One billion people working in freedom.

That purpose and vision acts as riverbanks that keep the organization slowly working together. If you're going to have those, if you don't have riverbanks, you're going to have a flood, right? You have to have a clear purpose and vision.

You create a climate of dialogue and listening and there's lots of trainings, lots of things out there to create open authentic dialogue and by doing that you're going to create trust. Then you have the transparency. Start adding the transparency as you build more trust and then all of these things start to build.

It isn't exactly linear how the principles are implemented but those are ones I recommend starting with, purpose and vision, dialogue, listening and transparency. Usually good spot to end is reflection and evaluation which closes the feedback loop.

What NixonMcInnes did is they have implemented these principles and over time they come up with practices to solve problems. As there's more trust they can have, not only open books but open salaries. As there's even more of that, the money gang answers even more. The happy bucket, that's not super scary or threatening.

But as you build that trust then you can get to Church of Fail, these more advanced mastery levels of democracy.

Nicholas: Are there any disadvantages or costs or risks in going for democratic workplace?

Traci: I ask CEOs of this all the time when I talk with them, the dozens and dozens of CEOs. I say, "So, what's the drawback? What's the risk, what's the cost," as you just said. They all just pause and say, "Gosh, the drawback?" It's depends how you look at it. I think it's a drawback, if you see it this way, that you have to grow as person. You have to be willing to grow as a person.

I once asked the CEO of Pandora Online Radio. I don't know if you have it over there but they are quite big in the US. Wonderful publicly traded company. It's on the WorlBlu certified list, I said, "You know, what kind of person do you need to be, to be a CEO of a democratic company?" And he said, "You can't have anything to prove." I thought that was very powerful.

If you're walking around with that chip on your shoulder, looking to go prove yourself, you're already operating from ego and that's going to make it very hard to be democratic. Then I said to him, "Well, what do you have to be? What kind of person do you have to be, to be an employee in a democratic company?" He said, "You can't have anything to prove."

I think it's not for everyone because not everyone wants to grow. Not everyone wants to learn how to communicate better. Not everyone wants to have to be accountable. Some people, you know what, maybe their lives are really busy and you just want a job, show up, do what you're told and go home and that's fine. That's perfectly fine but for others they want more and therefore they're going to thrive, yes?

Nicholas: I suppose some degree of democratic principle is good, full stop but obviously, a democratic culture in an organization is going to be more applicable to some situations, suitable for some people in some locations for some tasks and not in others. Do you have a really clear idea of where it works and what it doesn't? Where it thrives and where it's a mistake?

Traci: There's two situations where it doesn't work. It has nothing to do with industry. It has nothing to do with geography. It has to do with the number one, if their mindset is ready for it. You know you're ready for it if you can see the benefits of democracy in the workplace beyond command and control.

If you can see it at least intellectually, the heart can follow along with it so you can have both. If their mindset is completely closed it's not time. They're not going to be ready to embrace it. Now, the other part of this, people always say to me, "Well, you know, we are the exception? We are a manufacturing company? We're this, we're that?" This works in every industry, in every size, and in every country. The only time it's not going to work is in a battle, a war situation, if you're at war.

Companies aren't at war. They might like to think they are. They may think that they are that important but they're not. When you're in a war situation, I'm talking on the battlefields that's when you need command and control, you need the command and control model.

Even then, I've spoken at the US Naval Academy and when I gave a key-note address there to them on these ideas, all of them said, this is the future of warfare, this collaboration. I'm talking when you're in the heat of the battle, that's when you have to get control.

As far as I understand, really democracy works in every other situation.

Nicholas: Thank you. Lots of things come from that. In case I forget, I suppose what you're saying therefore is that I because people have to be ready for a democratic workplace in terms of their own values and level of consciousness, presumably, you're not going around trying to persuade people. It's more when they feel ready. You're laying out the vision of how it's possible. This is how you did it as opposed to trying to twist people's arms and push them in that direction.

Traci: That's right. The heart and mind has to be ready. It takes two things to build a democratic mindset, a democratic company: the mind-set and framework. There's a lot of great people out there teaching people how to have a mindset of self-worth and then where WorldBlu makes our contribution is with the framework.

The more that I get deeper and deeper into these ideas, I really realized that in order to believe in democracy you have to have a high estimate of your own self-worth and the worth of others. You need to believe that people are genuinely good.

185

If you think that people are genuinely bad or evil and needs to be controlled, these ideas aren't going to resonate with you.

Nicholas: That's one of the key problems people have isn't it? "We can't do that because …" I remember speaking to someone who works in a very hierarchical organization and I was trying to persuade him to become more empowering of his staff. I saw the way in which he bullied, disempowered and crushed the souls of all the people under him.

He was actually quite a good person. I thought quite a lot of him really, personally, and I tried to get him to see how he could really empower, really get the most out of people. In one line he gave me the answer, he said, "Do you realize, if I take my boot off their heads, they will take everything, they'll go wild." Basically his view was that the only thing between anarchy and criminality was force.

Traci: Right, yes. Unfortunately, a lot of people think that way and they're just wrong. They're just wrong. When you have a story in your head you're looking for ways to reinforce your story. The thing in that situation is he was the leader doing that to everyone else and very possibly others are doing that to him and so he just perpetuated essentially an abusive bullying cycle and it's unfortunate.

Now, the thing is that so many leaders, they have a sense of hidden pride that, "My people are scared of me." They derive a sense of power as well as importance by thinking that others are afraid of them.

Now, let's just look at this purely from a logical standpoint. Research shows, and you probably know this more than I do, Nick, coming from your background, that when we are afraid, when we are in the state of fear, the peripheries of the brain shut down and we become very myopic in what we see is possible.

You heard me tell the story but let's look at analogy. If you're a gazelle trying to run away from a cheetah that's chasing you on the African Savannah, you're afraid and there's only one thing you need to do. You don't need to sit and weigh your options and get everyone's buy in, you need to just run to save your life.

Presumably if the cheetah doesn't catch the gazelle and the gazelle gets away, what does it do, it shakes it off and moves on as it's not safe here anymore. But we run our companies in this fearful state and then command people to "Produce!" and "Be innovative!" and "Be creative! How can they? When the brain is full of fear, the constant fear has literally limited even how they're able to think. I don't even know how anyone can get away of that argument anymore. It's just absolutely insane from my point of view. I'm sorry but it is.

Nicholas: I believe, like you, that people are basically good and given the right environment to thrive and choose, choose to be very positive. However, in any human system, there's always issues of competition, of conflict. There would always be those that cheat, that push in, that freeload, that kind of thing happens.

How does accountability, governance and discipline work in democratic organization?

Traci: Freedom takes tremendous responsibility and accountability and it takes personal accountability and responsibility. The important thing is that when there are disciplinary problems, you don't punish the whole for the actions of a few.

What I've seen across democratic companies is they create mechanisms to handle the discipline. There's not always a lot of issues because other people feel untrusted and empowered, again, it's a positive reinforcement cycle.

Let me tell you a story, one of our WorldBlu certified democratic organization is a school. It's called the Link School and they're in Colorado. They're a small school, they are high school of about 20 students because they are highly experiential. They take the students on these trips all over the world to learn about the world and develop them as leaders and characters.

A very cool school. I wish I could have gotten to go there. It sounds really neat. They run the entire school democratically. In the mornings, they have meetings to make major decisions. The students, they do a consensus based voting. The students have just as much say as the staff. So they'll raise an issue and through thumb up, middle or down, they cast their vote. It has to consensus, they want everyone thumbs up or whatever to go forward.

I was just talking with one of the people at the school the other day because I'm writing about this in my book that's coming out next year and he told me that there had been a disciplinary problem with one of the students, one of the students had done something, I don't know what the details were. The staff felt that the student should be expelled and basically didn't make this decision on their own but they took it to the students and the students said, "No, that's too harsh to do to the student. We know more of the story than the staff does." They talked about it, talked about it, talked about it and they decided not to expel the student. As a result the student has gone through a tremendous character transformation and probably learned a lot more and evolved a lot more by being able to stay at the school knowing that their peers are standing by and helping them sort this out than just being expelled and booted out.

Nicholas: You mentioned the US Navy, I heard you previously speak about a democratic culture on a US Navy ship. I wonder if you could say a bit about that. How that works?

Traci: Yes. There's a warship called the USS Benfold and it was ran by Captain Michael Abrashoff. He's gone on to do write about how he ran the USS Benfold democratically.

Then, to this day, everyone wanted to be on that ship. There was a tremendous sense of loyalty. There is joy. I mean these guys, gals are out in the ocean for extended amounts of time, it can be miserable existence, you know? There's nowhere to go. You can't run away.

He ran this ship democratically. I think it also made a financial impact. Everyone wanted to be on his ship. It was a really special experience. I encourage your viewers and listeners to read an article about it at http://www.fastcompany.com/36897/agenda-grassroots-leadership

Nicholas: In Britain, some of the areas that badly need democratic culture introduced are our large state bureaucracies such as the National Health Service.

When I raise that sort of question with people, you get the same points that you've been talking about, the need to control, the need to prevent risk, stop bad things happening, the need to manage funds and so on.

One of the key arguments that always comes up is that, "This isn't a democracy. We have to ..." (laughing) Actually I'm laughing at the paradox of this; "this isn't a democracy because we have to account to the minister in the government who then has to stand up in parliament and say the cliché that systems are in place and fit for purpose." Then they run it top down, like a machine.

I know that you've done some work for the CIA in America which is, by definition, a state bureaucracy working on very secretive and highly sensitive things. In what way does an organization like that integrate a degree of democratic culture?

Traci: Well, it's a very interesting story about the CIA and it's probably not the story that you think but it's instructive for all of us. You're right, if we look at governments, here we are in arguably democratic societies and it's ironic that our state governments aren't necessarily running democratically day in and day out.

I lived in Washington DC for eight years and spent more than my fair share of time in government organizations and building with people trying to help them understand all of this. When I was in DC, two things happened with the CIA that was fascinating. One was I was invited to do a workshop with an emerging leader's group within the CIA.

These were around fifteen twenty-somethings, very bright, very smart folks. They wanted to serve their country at the CIA and I ran a workshop for them on how to operate things democratically.

They got very fired up. They took these ideas back to their bosses and wanted to implement them. As you might able to guess some managers were not very receptive to these ideas. One year later all but one person in this emerging leaders group have left the CIA.

They had seen what was possible. They saw that it wasn't going to be happening there and they left. I didn't know that was going to happen. That wasn't the goal but it says, a sobering sense that I think anyone needs to be alerted to, that the Gen X, Gen Y generations, they do not want to work in a command and control environment. They want to give more.

Now to the CIA's credit, I was invited back several years later to give a keynote address there about democracy and workplace and they listened to the ideas, that's as far as they've taken it at this time.

Hopefully they'll see the light but I'm pretty sure that government organization and academia are the last bastions of command and control.

Nicholas: Yes, it's interesting that you bring up generations there because I was looking through your website at the company's that you've accredited as democratic companies. It was really obvious that the CEOs of those companies and the big players were all, I supposed of our generation of … what are we generation X, Y? I don't know.

Traci: Well, I'm a borderline Gen X and Y. I'm not sure where you are. Are you Gen X? Are you Gen X?

Nicholas: 1970.

Traci: Well, I'll tell you what. It isn't. These aren't companies that are just run by 20 or 30 somethings though it might look like that. Many of the CEOs are in their 50s. Let me think, we should do the average age. You'd be surprised how many are in their 50s. I don't know about 60s. I can think of a couple that might be in their 60s. I don't know if anyone's older than that.

I think it's more a mindset than the age thing to be perfectly honest because I think it's a mindset of folks who are ready for it more than age. A psychographic more a demographic.

Nicholas: I believe in what you're doing but having tried it myself in lots of contexts I know that it can generate a lot of resistance and a very long list of reasons why we can't do this.

Now, obviously you've been all around the world and you have heard every single one of those. Are there any challenges that people put to you that you've struggled with, that you don't have an answer to at the moment?

Traci: Well, not really. You know, I should say, yes. I'll tell you because any challenge, I run workshops like this where I invite the participants and I say, "Write down your three biggest challenges you're facing right now" and this is after I taught them about the framework. Then I say, "Okay, now look at the principles and I want you to think about what principle of principles can help you solve this problem?"

Then what I want you to do is to write down the command and control way of solving that problem and then I want you to write down the democratic way of solving that problem. It's just a light bulb moment for people and they're like, "Oh my gosh, I didn't realize. I was totally coming from fear and here I can come from a greater sense of freedom and possibility."

I think all these problems are solvable in a democratic way. We just have to be more creative than we've been before.

Nicholas: If someone is reading is either a leader of a company or an organization or within an organization and likes what you're saying and thinks, "Yes, let's do it." How do they begin the transition to a more democratic workplace?

Traci: Absolutely. Well, what you need to do first is benchmark where you are as an organization. There's a couple of important points to bring out here. First of all, we are talking about the design of an organization, not just culture.

See, people often think that these ideas about how do you help the culture. It is about culture but culture grows out of design and with a WorldBlu principles, it's actually framework of design.

What you need to do is benchmark where are we in the continuum of a command and control design to a democratic design? We have our tool called the WorldBlu Scorecard that measures where an organization is on this continuum.

My recommendation is to you to come to us and get accessed. When you are assessed by the WorldBlu Scorecard, you can become a member of WorldBlu.

There's our certified memberships, these are organizations that are already democratic but they want to keep growing and learning. The other kind of membership is called "On The Path Membership," and we offer mastermind groups and learning opportunities for folks to come together.

Then once you're accessed and you're on the path then what we can do is look at in the 10 principles, where you're doing well, where can it be a little bit better and then we sit down and we really start to think through.

Okay, how can we move the needle on this? And you ask earlier they have to cost money? Of course not. It doesn't have to cost money. It's not like you need to hire a bunch of big consultants. This isn't about going and getting a football machine or be able to have a pony for people to ride when they're sitting in an office.

These are tweaks that you make along the way that you can start. You can implement the happy buckets tomorrow, something like that.

Nicholas: Moving towards the final questions, I'd like to get to the biggest picture. Obviously, in the context of Western Civilization we are unfortunately, during a period of recession, we don't know if it's coming to an end.

One of the things that people might say is, "Traci's idea is really lovely but let's wait until we're thriving and things really take off." It strikes me that actually the ideas that you're putting forward may actually be the source of creativity, productivity and new ideas that would leads out of recession.

Traci: You're right on the mark. Let me give you an example of that. Your readers might be thinking, "Oh, this only works in small companies." Well, no. Democracy works in very large companies and one of them is called HCL Technologies. They're a 90,000 employee company, $3 billion IT company based outside of Delhi. I've been there, spent time with them.

They're in 25 countries globally. They operated command and control for decades. In 2005, they brought in a new CEO, he'd actually gone worked in the company for 21 years, became CEO and he says, "I want to run this company democratically. I want to make this transition. His name is Vineet Nayar.

Now, so here he goes and makes it democratic. In 2005, is when they start making this change when we're it hit by the global recession, what do you do? Most people they're afraid, they clamped down and let's revert back to these old styles of leadership but that's not what they did.

During the recession they needed to find a way to save a hundred million dollars or they would have to let people go. What they did was they stayed in a space of freedom rather than fear. They stayed transparent. They went to their employees and they said, "We have to save a hundred million dollars or we're going to have to let people go. Will you help us think of ways that we can do this?"

They created a blog where people could submit ideas. Folks submitted hundred of ideas. They acted on 76 of those ideas and instead of saving a $100 million they saved $260 million and they didn't have to lay anybody off.

Now imagine what that did for morale? Look at how it helped them come through this recession, they're thriving, they're thriving financially now and they didn't have to hurt employee morale or anything like that.

I think this really can be a solid strategy from moving a company through the recession period and thriving.

Nicholas: What about ownership structure? If you're trying to create a democratic culture, does it matter whether people own the company, whether they have a stake in it?

Traci: What matters the most is the ownership mentality, that's what matters the most. There are ownership structures out there. ESOPs, Employee Owned Stock Options, co-ops and those are all wonderful ownership models. Actual legal ownership does not mean you necessarily have to a democratic design of the day of the day operations of a company or democratic culture.

Over here, United Airlines, people can own stock but United is not a democratic company. I think that can be one practice of the democratic principles but in and of itself doesn't guarantee democracy.

Nicholas: It's easy to see how a CEO or an owner might do this. What is someone to do who finds himself in a command and control type, fear based or power based organization and they really want the freedom and the latitude and they can see how things can be done better and so one but they're getting resistance from the structure around them and all the usual long list of reasons why we can't do this?

Like your CIA people, you can just leave and go somewhere else but, certainly in Britain, some of our bureaucracies control the industry. For example, as a doctor, the state system has 97 percent of the jobs. Really people can't really leave without leaving the profession.

If someone is in that situation, what can they do to influence it for the better?

Traci: Yes, I wrote an article about this for Yahoo Hot Jobs. I can send you to article if you email me. But I think, you know, this is a hard situation, if you can't leave. And you need to work it out.

I recommend that, you know, the Gandhi saying, "Be the change that you wish to see." You have to do your best to model the democratic behavior and do your best in your own small way to find ways to implement the principles maybe on your team, on your department or just in your day to day interactions and just be that light and hold the space for these ideas.

Slowly and surely people will notice. Just focus on yourself if you can't focus on making the big change. Hopefully that can elevate you. There are a lot of great books out that I really recommend. Ricardo Semler's book about Semco is called Maverick or The Seven Day Weekend. He's sort of the grandfather of organizational democracy.

Although the hard thing is you read these books and you start seeing what's possible and you're like, "Aaaah!" You can't stay in this. But my heart goes out to everyone who's in that position.

Nicholas: Great. Very final question Traci. If that one billion people take up your ideas and leaving in a democratic culture in their workplaces can you fast forward to that time and describe to us what it would be like to live that way.

Traci: I love that question. Yes, I think what we're going to see is a world of people who are happier and who feel a greater sense of joy, lasting joy. They're going to be more calm, they're going to be able to come home and enjoy their families and not kick the dog because they're frustrated at work. You're going to see a lot more profitability. I think more money. I think you're going to see more prosperity and a greater sense of peace.

Nicholas: If anyone wants to get in touch with you or have a look at your website, could you say what the best address would be?

Traci: Yes, www.WorldBlu.com. We're called WorldBlu because blue is universally recognized as the color of freedom and right there at WorldBlu.com there's a contact page, my direct email is on there, my team member's emails are on there and you can reach out to us directly and we'd be happy to correspond with you.

Nicholas: Fantastic. Thank you so much, Traci.

Traci: Thanks for having me.

Nicholas: Wishing you the best of luck.

Traci: Thanks for having me Nicholas. I really appreciate it.

Other Books in the Series

The Future of Western Civilization series is available in four books in paperback and ebook. Each interview is also available as a separate ebook. You will find them on the main online book retailers.

www.FutureofWesternCivilization.com

Future of Western Civilization Series 1, Book 2

The West is Best
Insights from the PR Man to the Stars

Evolutionary Enlightenment
Living from your Creative Impulse

Renaissance 2
Catalyzing the Second Renaissance.

Positive Patriotism
The Evolving British

The Master Code
The Theory that Explains Everything

Future of Western Civilization Series 1, Book 3

Generational Cycles
Predicting the Future

Catalyzing Change
Engaging Emergence

Successful Nations
Harnessing the Aspirations of the People

Resurrecting Christianity
Rising to the Challenges of a Complex World

German Identity & Patriotism
Healing the Wounds, Integrating the Shadow.

Compassionate Healthcare
Re-humanising Medicine

New Money
The Evolution of Finance

Future of Western Civilization Series 1, Book 4

Unleashing Human Potential
Alignment, Energetics and Connection

Wise Democracy
Discovering Solutions to Intractable Problems

Mindfulness
Applications for Leaders and Clinicians

Evolutionary Leadership
Conscious Leadership in an Age of Transition

The Future of Europe
A View from Inside the European Union

Ending the Culture War
A Devoted Conservative and a Die-hard Liberal Make Friends

The Future of Western Civilization Progress Report

Contact & Social Media

Thank you so much for reading the Future of Western Civilization. Please do get in touch to share your comments. Please visit the websites below.

www.FutureofWesternCivilization.com

www.nicholasbeecroft.com

http://www.facebook.com/groups/438696922812104/

http://twitter.com/Future_of_West

http://www.linkedin.com/groups?gid=4400956

Write a review

If you really enjoyed the book and the series, then please do tell your friends, share on social media and do please post reviews on Amazon, Goodreads, Kobo, Barnes & Noble, Sony, Smashwords etc. It'll help others decide whether to get a copy for themselves. If you have found any typos, awful grammar or anything else I can put right, please email me directly and I'll do so.

Best wishes,
Nicholas

www.ingramcontent.com/pod-product-compliance
Lightning Source LLC
Chambersburg PA
CBHW070901290526
45795CB00001B/193